THE DARKER FACE OF THE EARTH

PRAISE FOR

THE DARKER FACE OF THE EARTH

A major American play... With skill that approaches a celestial gift, Dove blends form, subject and content.

—*The Mail Tribune*

[Dove's] first venture into playwriting has produced an enormously powerful and beautiful work. The themes are intricate, the main characters full-bodied and the language—oh, the language—nothing short of stunning.

—*CurtainUp*

Playwright Dove merges folklore, voodoo ritual and biblical analogy with biting social commentary. The action is suspenseful, the dialogue picturesque.

—*Variety*

The Darker Face of the Earth marks a considerable achievement... This powerful exploration of sexual and racial tensions is assembled in an imaginative realm, with few technical requirements.

—*Harvard Review*

Lushly written, ingeniously plotted, drenched in antebellum atmosphere, *The Darker Face of the Earth* has lots of soul.

—*The Guardian (England)*

Black theatre takes a big step forward.

—*The Stage*

Sophocles and slavery come together with bitter poignancy... By connecting the issue of slavery to one of the most fundamental Greek tragedies, *The Darker Face of the Earth* draws its own inescapable conclusion about the impact of an immoral institution.

—*The Balitmore Sun*

A strong and ambitious piece of work... [Dove] does one of the hardest things to do onstage, something maybe only a poet could—she creates in Augustus a living metaphor... [He] is not only Oedipus here, but Hamlet and Moses, and all the Greek heroes unlucky enough to be half-mortal and half-God... Throughout the play, the transference of the legend from ancient Greece to the antebellum South works surprisingly well... [Dove's] scenes are shaped with ease and grace; her dialogue, even when poetic, is expressive; and she has a vivid sense of character.

—*The Washington Post*

...the play's selectivity of incident, judicious sparseness, clean lines, even dignified tone and simple staging keep it operating successfully as a modernization of the classic Greek tragic mode.

—*The Women's Review of Books*

...[this] play begs to be staged. One can dream a little and wish that it could be produced in every city, every school in the country.

—*The Times* (Trenton, NJ)

[Rita Dove's] riveting and accomplished play... should have a permanent place in the repertoire of the American theater.

—*The Star-Ledger*

WORKS BY RITA DOVE

POETRY

On the Bus with Rosa Parks
W.W. Norton, 1999

Mother Love
W.W. Norton, 1995

Selected Poems
Pantheon / Vintage, 1993

Grace Notes
W.W. Norton, 1989

Thomas and Beulah
Carnegie-Mellon, 1986

Museum
Carnegie-Mellon, 1983

The Yellow House on the Corner
Carnegie-Mellon, 1980

FICTION

Through the Ivory Gate, a novel
Pantheon, 1992

Fifth Sunday, short stories
Callaloo Fiction Series, 1985

DRAMA

The Darker Face of the Earth
1st edition, Story Line Press, 1994;
Completely revised 2nd edition,
Story Line Press, 1996, and
Oberon Books, London, 1999

"The Siberian Village," a one-act play
(in *Callaloo*, Vol. 14/2, 1991)

NON-FICTION

The Poet's World
The Library of Congress, 1995

THE DARKER FACE

OF THE EARTH

A PLAY
BY RITA DOVE

THIRD EDITION

STORY LINE PRESS

Ashland, Oregon

FIRST STAGE PRODUCTION:
Oregon Shakespeare Festival (OSF), Ashland, Oregon, July 27, 1996
with the support of a major grant from the W. Alton Jones Foundation.

All performance and audiovisual rights are with the author. For production permission, contact in writing: Rita Dove, Department of English 219, Bryan Hall, University of Virginia, Charlottesville, VA 22903. For production and acting copies, contact the publisher.

Published by Story Line Press, Inc., Three Oaks Farm, PO Box 1240, Ashland, OR 97520-0055
Printed in the United States of America

This publication was made possible thanks in part to the generous support of the Nicholas Roerich Museum, the Andrew W. Mellon Foundation, the National Endowment for the Arts, US West Foundation and individual contributors.

LIBRARY OF CONGRESS CATALOGING-IN-PUBLICATION DATA
Dove, Rita.
  The darker face of the earth: a play / by Rita Dove.—3rd ed.
    p. cm.
  ISBN 1-885266-94-4 (pbk.)
    1. South Carolina—History—1775–1865—Drama. 2. Women plantation owners—Drama. 3. Mothers and sons—Drama. 4. Plantation life—Drama. 5. Afro-Americans—Drama. 6. Slaves—Drama. I. Title.

PS3554.0884 D68 2000
812' .54—dc21   00-059573

ACKNOWLEDGMENTS

First and foremost I would like to thank my husband, Fred Viebahn, for his encouragement and help during all the stages of my work on this play—from the moment decades ago in our sun-drenched apartment at Mishkenot Sha'ananim, Jersualem, when I first told him my idea, through the years the first draft spent relegated to the bottom of a drawer, to the day Story Line Press offered to publish the manuscript, and finally to the play's realization on stage. I am indebted to my daughter Aviva, who—in the clear wisdom of youth—never let her love for the play blind her to the wobbles and bloopers so unerringly detected by her laser eye.

I am also grateful to Robert McDowell of Story Line Press for his vision and enthusiasm and to Cynthia White, former director of play development at Oregon Shakespeare Festival, for her unflagging support, which lead directly to the first full stage production in 1996. Of the many people who were involved in earlier renderings I can mention only the principal players: Jennifer Nelson not only brought her inspired direction to a three-week workshop at the Oregon Shakespeare Festival in 1994 (my first behind-the-stage theatre experience), but directed staged readings at the Round House in Silver Springs, Maryland, and at the Roundabout Theatre on Broadway (with Edgar Lansbury as producer); director Ricardo Khan's and dramaturg Sydné Mahone's passionate insights propelled a staged reading at Crossroads Theatre in New Brunswick, New Jersey; and Derek Walcott directed a superb case by lending his genius to a very poetic and dramatic reading at the 92nd Street Y in New York City.

CAST

Female slaves:
PHEBE
PSYCHE, in her mid teens
SCYLLA, pronounced "Skilla"
TICEY, a house slave
DIANA, a young girl about 12 years old
SLAVE WOMAN/NARRATOR

Male slaves:
HECTOR, an African
ALEXANDER
SCIPIO, pronounced "Sippio"
AUGUSTUS NEWCASTLE, a mulatto

The whites:
AMALIA JENNINGS LAFARGE
LOUIS LAFARGE, Amalia's husband
DOCTOR, in his fifties
JONES, the overseer, in his thirties

The black conspirators:
LEADER
BENJAMIN SKEENE
HENRY BLAKE

Other slaves and conspirators

The Darker Face of the Earth was first performed at the Oregon Shakespeare Festival in Ashland, Oregon, USA, on 27 July 1996, under the direction of Ricardo Khan and with the following cast:

PHEBE .... B. W. Gonzalez

PSYCHE .... Gina Daniels

SCYLLA .... Tamu Gray

TICEY .... Michelle Blackmon

DIANA .... Nadine Griffith

SLAVE WOMAN/NARRATOR .... Johanna Jackson

HECTOR .... Thomas Byrd

ALEXANDER .... J. P. Phillips

SCIPIO .... Davon Russell

AUGUSTUS .... Ezra Knight

AMALIA .... Elizabeth Norment

LOUIS .... Mark Murphey

DOCTOR .... Dennis Robertson

JONES .... Paul Vincent O'Connor

LEADER .... Tyrone Wilson

BENJAMIN .... August Gabriel

HENRY .... Kevin Kenerly

SLAVES/CONSPIRATORS .... The ensemble

DRUMMERS .... Russ Appleyard/Craig Goodmond

Time

> Prologue: about 1820.
> Acts I and II: twenty years later.

Place

> The action takes place in antebellum South Carolina, on
> the Jennings Plantation and in its environs.

The characters of Psyche and Diana, as well as the Doctor and Jones, can be played by the same actors, as long as it is made clear to the audience that they are different people.

On occasion, the slaves comment upon the play somewhat in the manner of a Greek chorus. Individual characters are bound by time and circumstance; the chorus of slaves is more detached and omni-present. By moving and speaking in a ritualized manner, they provide vocal and percussive counterpoint to the action. The slave woman who occasionally steps forward as the narrator, is quietly present in all slave scenes.

This play is for my daughter

Aviva Chantal Tamu Dove-Viebahn.

PROLOGUE

Lights rise on the big house, revealing the porch, AMALIA's bedroom, LOUIS' study and the hallway.

HECTOR, a slave in his early twenties, is standing on the porch, looking up at a second-story window. PHEBE, a slave girl in her early teens, runs onstage; she is coming from the basement kitchen. Skinny and electric, she is chuckling to herself.

PHEBE

What some people won't do
for attention! Shore,
he's alright-looking—
but that ain't qualification enough
for the big white bed
in the big white house!

Laughs at her own wit; then, skipping in a circle, sings.

Stepped on a pin, the pin bent,
and that's the way the story went!

PSYCHE

(Offstage.)

Phebe! Phebe! You up there?

PHEBE

Here I am, Psyche!

PSYCHE enters. She is petite, shy; though not much older than PHEBE, she treats her like a little sister.

PSYCHE

You shouldn't go running off
by yourself, chile.

PHEBE	Look: Hector on the porch.
	She giggles and points to HECTOR.
PSYCHE	Leave him be, poor soul.
PHEBE	Aw, Psyche! Anybody crazy enough to be standing there, thinking he—
PSYCHE	Shush now, chile!
PHEBE	*PHEBE shrugs, hums and skips again. The other SLAVES straggle in, tired from the day's work, whispering among themselves, a suppressed excite- ment in their manner.*
PHEBE	What took you all so long? Slower than a pack of lame turtles.
ALEXANDER	*(A dignified man in his forties.)*
	We all ain't quite so spry as you, gal.
PHEBE	Shh!
	Everyone freezes.
	I thought I heard something.
PSYCHE	Aw, girl—
SCYLLA	*(A tall dark woman in her twenties.)*
	Must be a hard birthin'.
PSYCHE	I sure hope she makes it. Her mama—

SCYLLA	Her mama was the weakest excuse for a woman ever dropped on this earth. But this one—
	With a significant look to the window.
	this one got her daddy in her.
ALEXANDER	Nothing but trouble, I tell you. Nothing but trouble.
	Lights up on AMALIA's bedroom. AMALIA JEN-NINGS LAFARGE lies in a canopy bed, a thickly swaddled babe in her arms. She is an attractive white woman, close to 20 years old, who exhibits more intelligence and backbone than is generally credited to a Southern belle. The DOCTOR, an older whiskered gentleman, is pacing the floor. AMALIA, though exhausted, appears amused.
AMALIA	Well, Doctor, isn't he beautiful?
DOCTOR	This is serious, Amalia! If the niggers get wind of this—
	AMALIA begins humming a lullaby to the baby.
AMALIA	Don't get melodramatic, Doctor; you'll frighten my son. See?
	Baby raises a cry; AMALIA continues to hum while the DOCTOR keeps pacing. Among the SLAVES, SCYLLA stands up, clutching her stomach.
SCYLLA	Oh! Oh!
OTHERS	What is it, Scylla? What is it?
SCYLLA	It's out in the world.

The SLAVES look at her in fear.

ALEXANDER   Lord have mercy.

The SLAVES gather around SCYLLA as she tries to straighten up but cannot. HECTOR's gaze is still fixed on the window. AMALIA's husband rushes into the bedroom. LOUIS LAFARGE is a handsome man in his twenties. The DOCTOR holds him back.

LOUIS   Doctor—

DOCTOR   Everything's fine. Just go on back outside.

LOUIS   Can't a man see his own child?

Tears himself free and rushes over to the bed.

AMALIA   What, Louis—struck dumb?

LOUIS   My God!

AMALIA   Isn't he a fine strapping boy?

DOCTOR   This is unnatural.

LOUIS   Who did this to you?
                 I'll have him whipped to a pulp—

AMALIA   (*Hissing.*)

                 So it's alright for you
                 to stroll out by the cabins
                 any fine night you please? Ha—
                 the Big White Hunter with his scrawny whip!

LOUIS   That tears it!

20

DOCTOR   Quiet! They might hear.

LOUIS   I'll kill her!

*LOUIS lunges at AMALIA; the DOCTOR
restrains him.*

DOCTOR   Hold it, sir! Calm yourself!

AMALIA   (*To the DOCTOR.*)

Daddy tried to keep me from
marrying him—but I was in love
with riding boots and the smell
of shaving cream and bourbon.
I was in love with a cavalryman
and nothing could stop me,
not even Daddy!

*To LOUIS, who is being forced into an armchair
by the DOCTOR.*

But not even Daddy
suspected where you would seek
your satisfaction.
It was your right
to pull on those riding boots
and stalk little slave girls.
God knows what you do to them
in the name of ownership.

*Depleted from the bravado she has mustered,
AMALIA bends over the baby so they won't see
her exhaustion. LOUIS, still sitting in the arm-
chair, grabs the DOCTOR by the shirt and pulls
him down to his level.*

LOUIS	Get rid of it! Destroy the bastard!
DOCTOR	My charge is to preserve life, Mr LaFarge, not to destroy it.
LOUIS	What's the matter? Aren't you a man?
DOCTOR	(*Scathingly; a fierce whisper.*) My manhood isn't the question here. Do you want your business smeared across the whole county? Think for a minute: What have we got here? A fresh slave. New property. And you're in need of a little spare change, aren't you? I understand the cards haven't been much in your favor lately.
LOUIS	What are you trying to say, Doctor?
AMALIA	Stop your whispering, gentlemen. No one's going to touch this baby!
LOUIS	You can be sure I'll never touch you again!
AMALIA	That's one blessing.
DOCTOR	Is this baby worth destroying your life? *Pulling LOUIS aside.* Give me a minute alone with her. I'll make her see reason. Go on, now. *He shoves the reluctant LOUIS out of the door, then moves quickly to the window to peek out on the slaves below. Among the SLAVES, excitement reigns as SCYLLA hobbles over to HECTOR, whose eyes are still fixed on the bedroom window.*

PHEBE	(*To PSYCHE.*)
	Scylla gonna be alright?
PSYCHE	(*Sees the curtains move.*)
	Hush chile!
	Pointing to the window.
	Something's stirring.
	The SLAVES look up to the window and freeze. The DOCTOR returns to AMALIA, who is singing to the baby.
DOCTOR	You can cease your motherly blandishments, Amalia. He's gone.
AMALIA	I knew you were good for something besides tonics and botched surgeries, Doctor!
DOCTOR	Oh, you're mighty clever, Miss Jennings— no wonder your marriage is a disappointment. Hell, your daddy saw it coming; he worried about you. How many times did he have to haul you back from the fields, kicking and scratching like a she-cat?
AMALIA	And just who was I supposed to play with—the pigs and the chickens? Daddy could run a plantation but he didn't know the first thing about raising a daughter. All morning he'd teach me to calculate inventory, but he expected his slippers darned come evening! And when I refused, off I went— to finishing school and the Charleston society balls.
	Lights up on LOUIS, sitting on the bed in his room, head in hands.

LOUIS

Spare change. Spare change!
How they all smirk! I know what they're thinking.
"Louis sure slipped into a silk-lined purse!"

Takes a swig from a flask in his jacket.

Damn his blasted Hippocratic oath!

Paces, agitated; then stops, an idea dawning.

That's it! Of course.
Doctor, I'll save you the trouble.

He rummages in drawers; lights up on AMALIA's room.

AMALIA

When I came home from Charleston
with my brand new dashing husband,
Daddy had the slaves line the path
from the gate to the front porch;
and as we walked through the ranks
each one stepped up with
the nosegays they had picked—
awkward bunches of wildflowers.
I was laughing, gathering up bouquets
and tossing them to Louis.

We were almost to the porch
when suddenly there appeared this...
this rose. One red rose,
thrust right into the path so we had to stop.
I recognised him right away.
We hadn't seen each other
since Daddy sent him to the fields.
We used to sneak out to Mama's
old cutting garden; it was overgrown
and the roses had run particularly wild!

Softly, remembering.

One day he covered me in rose petals,
then blew them off, one by one.
He'd never seen anything like them
back in Africa.

In wonder.

And there he stood, all grown up,
with one red rose held out
like it was a piece of him
growing straight from his fist.
"What a lovely tribute to the bride!" I said—

Shaking off the spell of the memory.

then passed it to Louis to tuck in with the rest.

DOCTOR   I suppose there's no sense in talking about
          your duty to the institution of marriage.

AMALIA   I made one mistake—Louis.
          I don't have to go on living it.

DOCTOR   Oh, there's where you're wrong.
          Amalia Jennings. Some mistakes
          don't right themselves that easy.
          Some mistakes you live with until you die.

          *Lights up on LOUIS in his bedroom as he emerges
          from the back of the wardrobe with a pair of spurs,
          still trailing red ribbons.*

LOUIS   (*Sneering.*)

          There they are!
          Amalia's Christmas present—

fancy new riding spurs!
Won't they make a special
"christening" present
for the little bitty baby
to tuck in with its blanket!

*LOUIS chuckles as he pockets the spurs and leaves
the room. Lights up on SLAVES. HECTOR
stretches his hand toward the window and speaks,
as if trying to remember.*

HECTOR   Eshu Elewa...

PHEBE   What's he saying?

PSYCHE   Something surely gone wrong.

Lights up on AMALIA and DOCTOR.

DOCTOR   How long do you think it will take
                before your slaves begin to speak back?
                To botch the work and fall ill
                with mysterious ailments? Then
                who will help you—Louis?
                An overseer who knows his mistress
                is tainted with slave funk? In a bad year,
                how much will you have to beg
                to get a tab at the store?
                Who will you invite to tea, Amalia—
                your dashing blackamoor?

AMALIA   What a convenient morality, Doctor.

DOCTOR   I'm just trying to save
                your daddy's good name.
                As for your precious little bundle—

26

how long do you think he'll last
with Louis feeling as he does?
How long before your child
accidentally drowns
or stumbles under a horse's hooves?
You can't keep him, Amalia;
if you truly love him,
you cannot keep him.

AMALIA buries her face in the pillow and begins to weep.

DOCTOR   I know a family who handles
these... delicate matters.
They'll raise him and arrange for sale
when it's time.

AMALIA clutches the baby to her.

He'll be treated well. I'll make sure of that.

Silence. AMALIA stares at the baby.

AMALIA   Give me a little more time!

DOCTOR   You had nine months.

The baby makes a noise; she lays him on her breast.

AMALIA   There's no way back, is there?

*HECTOR falls to his knee and cries out;
SCYLLA tries to restrain him.*

HECTOR   Eshu Elewa ogo gbogbo!

SCYLLA	No, Hector.
ALEXANDER	Lord help him.
PSYCHE	Lord help us all.

Lights up on AMALIA's bedroom; there's a knock at the door.

DOCTOR
There he is. Now:
I'll take the baby to Charleston tonight.
You must play the wronged wife.
No matter the truth—whatever the truth—
this affair was an act of revenge,
your retaliation to Louis' philandering.
But you won't keep the child
to taunt him, oh, no! Instead,
you'll forgive and forget...and show him
how to turn a profit besides.

*AMALIA stares at the DOCTOR with disgust.
The DOCTOR opens the door.*

Come in, sir.

LOUIS enters, glaring.

This is a damned tricky situation,
but I think I've sorted it out.

*Warming up to his role as the arbiter of responsibil-
ity and morality; pacing self-importantly.*

Out of rage and sorrow over
your philandering behaviour, Louis,
Amalia has responded in kind.
An extreme vindication, true,
and utterly reprehensible—unless
we remember what prompted it

in the first place. Are we agreed?

Both LOUIS and AMALIA are silent.

As for the bastard child...

Pauses for effect.

Amalia has agreed to let it go.
I have a friend in Charleston
who likes raising slaves
from the ground up. He's familiar
with the story of the distraught wife
confronted with the evidence
of a husband's wandering lust.

LOUIS   No! I won't take the blame!

DOCTOR   No one need know it's come
                     from the Jennings Plantation.

LOUIS   What about the niggers? They're out
                     on the lawn, waiting for news.

DOCTOR   We'll say the poor soul expired
                     directly after birth, took one breath
                     and died. I've taken the body away.

LOUIS   No funeral? Niggers love funerals.

DOCTOR   No—Amalia didn't want a funeral.
                     They'll believe it. They have no choice.

                     To AMALIA.

                     You better make sure the father
                     keeps his mouth shut.

AMALIA   (*Haunted.*)

                     Who would believe him?

LOUIS	I must say, your ingenuity is impressive, Doctor. It's what I'd call a "master" plan.
	Pointing to the sideboard where AMALIA keeps an oblong wicker sewing basket, trimmed with red velvet rosettes and lined in blue silk.
	That basket—surely you'd donate your sewing basket to the cause, Amalia? It would fit so nicely behind the good doctor's saddle.
DOCTOR	(*Examines the basket.*)
	Yes, that will do.
	LOUIS places the basket next to the bed.
AMALIA	Go tell them. Spread the sad tidings.
	She says this with difficulty. DOCTOR and LOUIS exit as AMALIA carefully unwraps the baby and inspects him, top to toe. Lights up on the DOCTOR and LOUIS in the hall; TICEY, a house slave in her forties, approaches them.
TICEY	How's Miss Jennings, suh? The baby sure sounds like a big one!
DOCTOR	(*Harshly.*)
	The baby's dead.
TICEY	Dead? But I heard it cry!
DOCTOR	He cried out once. Poor little thing had no more breath left.

TICEY   Now, if that ain't the strangest thing...

LOUIS   (*Sharply.*)

                 What's so strange about it?
                 The baby just up and died.
                 Happens all the time.

DOCTOR   Look at you, standing here arguing
                 like a fool hen, while your mistress
                 is in there crying her eyes out!

                 Shaking his head.

                 Now go on out to those niggers—
                 I know you got them waiting by the porch.
                 Tell them there'll be no wailing and moaning,
                 no singing or mighty sorry, Ma'am.
                 Miss Jennings wants no funeral.
                 Miss Jennings wants to forget.
                 Go on now, scat!

TICEY   Yassuh. Sorry suh.

                 *TICEY exits. During the following scene she ap-
                 proaches PSYCHE, takes her aside, whispering. At
                 PSYCHE's shocked reaction, the SLAVES, except for
                 HECTOR and SCYLLA, crowd around. TICEY re-
                 treats back into the house while the other SLAVES
                 lower their heads, softly humming in a frozen tableau.
                 HECTOR falls to his knees; SCYLLA stands over
                 him, severely bent.*

                 *In the bedroom, AMALIA embraces the baby one last
                 time.*

AMALIA   This basket will be your cradle now.
                 Blue silk for my prince, and a canopy of roses!
                 Don't be afraid: it's warm inside.

AMALIA (con't.)   *Places first a small blanket, then the baby inside, takes one last look, nearly breaking down.*

I dreamed you before you came;
now I must remember you before you go.

Collects herself as she wraps the blanket around the baby and closes the lid.

DOCTOR   Let's get this over with.

LOUIS   Go ahead. Doctor, I—I'll wait here.

The DOCTOR enters the bedroom.

DOCTOR   Ready?

AMALIA averts her head, thrusts the basket at him.

I wasn't sure you had it in you,
but I'll say one thing, Amalia Jennings—
you are your father's daughter.

DOCTOR exits with the basket. AMALIA buries her face in the pillows.

DOCTOR   I best be on my way.

LOUIS   You have a hard ride ahead of you, Doctor.
Would you care for a bit of bourbon
to warm your way?

DOCTOR   (*Slightly surprised.*)

Why yes, that would do nicely.
Just put it with my things.

As the DOCTOR turns to get his coat and hat, LOUIS slips the spurs in the sewing basket, under the blanket, then puts the flask into the DOCTOR's bag.

LOUIS

There, you're all set—
best medicine made by man!

DOCTOR

It's over, Louis. Nothing left but to forget.

LOUIS

Have a pleasant journey, Doctor.

DOCTOR

I will try.

Lights go out as the DOCTOR exits. The SLAVE WOMAN/NARRATOR steps forward. During the NARRATOR's speech, the SLAVES go about their tasks, humming as the lights slowly warm to sunrise and the stage begins to transmogrify, simulating the passing of 20 years: a tree growing, the big house being enlarged, etc.

NARRATOR

Take a little seed,
put it in the ground;
the seed takes root,
sends its tendrils down

till the sapling shoots
its branches high—
roots piercing ground,
limbs touching sky.

Now the mighty tree
is twenty years tall;
seed become king,
and the king takes all.

ACT ONE

Scene 1

The cotton fields. DIANA, a slave girl, collapses. SCIPIO, a young slave working nearby, hesitates.

SCIPIO

Move it gal, or
you'll feel it later!

PHEBE

(*Helping her up.*)

Lift in your knees, Diana;
try not to think about your blood.
Tomorrow's Sunday—
tomorrow you can rest.

DIANA

(*Derisively.*)

Blessed be the Sabbath!

PHEBE

The child's too young to tote that sack.
She should be helping in the kitchen,
like we was raised.

ALEXANDER

You was raised with Massa Jennings,
Phebe—and he been gone these twenty-some years.
You know his daughter got other ideas.

PHEBE

She grow eviller year for year.

ALEXANDER

Ain't right, a woman
running a plantation like that.

SCIPIO	Woman? She's more man than woman.
PHEBE	And more devil than man.
ALEXANDER	Ever since she lost that child.
PHEBE	Oh, Alexander!
ALEXANDER	White folks feel a loss as much as we do— it's just that they ain't used to losing. I tell you, Miss Amalia went crazy in the head the day she lost that baby boy.
SCYLLA	That's not the way Ticey told it.
	SCYLLA is severely bent over and walks with a limp. Her gaze is fearful.
ALEXANDER	(*To DIANA.*) Nowadays old Ticey don't tell us field niggers nothing. But that night she come from the Big House and say to Psyche...
PHEBE	That's enough, Alexander.
DIANA	Phebe, what was my mama like?
PHEBE	Chile, you heard that story a hundred times. Ain't no different now, just 'cause you turned to a woman yourself.
DIANA	Please, Phebe.

PHEBE   (*Tenderly, as she resumes picking cotton.*)

                Psyche was the sister I never had.
                Why, she pulled me offa trouble
                so many times, I thought her hand
                had growed to my shoulder!

DIANA   (*Begins to cry.*)

                I wish I'd a known her.

PHEBE   Childbirth can kill the strongest woman.

ALEXANDER   Or kill the child.

SCYLLA   You still believe the white folks?
                That baby weren't born dead.
                Ticey heard it cry. I seen the doctor
                carry it off in a basket, but
                it weren't dead. I felt it kick.

DIANA   (*Wiping her tears.*)

                The baby kicked?

ALEXANDER   Scylla got her powers that night.

SCYLLA   (*Staring at DIANA, who shrinks back.*)

                The child was born alive!
                I know. I felt it.

PHEBE   Scylla...

SCYLLA   The veil was snatched from my eyes—
                and over the hill I saw

SCYLLA (con't.)	bad times a-coming. Bad times coming over the hill on mighty horses, horses snorting as they galloped through slave cabin and pillared mansion, horses whinnying as they trampled everything in their path. Like a thin black net the curse settled over the land.
DIANA	What curse?
PHEBE	Don't pay her no mind.
SCYLLA	The curse touched four people.
DIANA	*(Getting scared.)* Who were they? Who were the four people?
SLAVES	Black woman, black man, white woman, white man.
SCYLLA	When the curse came I stood up to meet it, and it knocked me to the ground.
SLAVES	Black woman.
SCYLLA	My womb dried up, but the power churned in me.
PHEBE	We best get back to pickin'. No tellin' where Jones got off to—
SCIPIO	Same place he always "gets off to" —that clump of timothy at the spring where he's tucked his whiskey!

SCYLLA appears to be in a trance; SLAVES
accompany her in a syncopated whisper.

SCYLLA

Hector, son of Africa—
stolen from his father's hut,
sold on the auction block!

SLAVES

Black man.

SCYLLA

Hector was a slave in the fields
until Miss Amalia took him up
to the house. He followed her
like her own right shoe.
When she felt faint,
he brought her iced lemon water;
when she started to show,
he helped her up the stairs;
when the baby kicked,
he soothed her.
But when her time came
he had to stand out by the porch
like the rest of us.
And when Ticey brought the news
Hector fell to his knees
and ate dirt like a worm.
Now he lives alone
and catches snakes in the swamp.

SLAVES

Black woman, black man—
both were twisted
when the curse came over the hill.

SCYLLA

While the slave turned to grief,
the master turned to business.
Miss Amalia hiked up her skirts
and pulled on man's boots.

SLAVES	White woman.
SCYLLA	And Massa Louis... Massa Louis took off his riding breeches—
SLAVES	White man.
SCYLLA	— and shut himself upstairs. Some nights you can see him out on the balcony, staring at the sky: he has machines to measure the stars.
SLAVES	Black woman, black man; white woman, white man!
SCYLLA	Four people touched by the curse: but the curse is not complete.
DIANA	I'm scared.
PHEBE	(*In spite of herself.*)
	Did you have to tell her so much, Scylla? She's just a child.
SCYLLA	She's old enough to know, and you're old enough to know better.
PHEBE	I was there, too. I didn't see no horses comin' over the hill. You just crumpled up like a leaf.
	AMALIA enters unseen in riding clothes, whip in hand.
SCYLLA	I can strike you down like lightning, Phebe. I can send demons mightier—

AMALIA	What's this?
PHEBE	How—how de do, Miss Amalia! We was just trying to figure out what to do with Diana here.
AMALIA	She seems healthy enough to me— good stock, young and fresh.
PHEBE	(*Motioning for DIANA to look sicker.*)
	She fell out something awful. It don't look like she feel too good—
AMALIA	You aren't here to play doctor, Phebe. Where is that Jones? Jones!
	JONES is nowhere to be seen. Impatient, AMALIA prods DIANA with the whip stock.
	Lazy pack! I swear I've seen cows smarter than you! Jones!
JONES	(*Rushes in, wiping his mouth with his sleeve.*)
	Yes, Miss Jennings?
AMALIA	Get these niggers in line! Drink on your own time.
JONES	Yes'm.
AMALIA	I'll see you this evening up at the house.
JONES	Yes, Ma'am. I'll be there, Ma'am!
	She strides off; JONES mops his brow with a huge handkerchief.

JONES (con't.)   Goddamn niggers, gotta watch you
                   every second! Get that gal back on her feet!

                   Cracking his whip.

                   Keep your mouths shut and your hands picking
                   or you'll feel my lash, sick or not!

                   Watches them resume work; then exits.

SCYLLA   I believe it's about time for you
                   to pay me a little visit, Phebe.
                   Tomorrow evening—
                   after the moon's set.

PHEBE   Aw, Scylla, I didn't mean nothing—

SCYLLA   It'll be pitch dark. Take care
                   you don't trip on the way.

                   Blackout.

Scene 2

The big house, the parlor and LOUIS' study.

LOUIS is visible at the window of his study, peering through a telescope at the stars; he occasionally takes notes or sips his brandy.

AMALIA sits at the desk in the parlor; JONES stands in front of her.

JONES

Sorry about this afternoon, Ma'am.
That little gal seemed real sick, you know.

AMALIA

Mr. Jones, I am aware you come fresh
from the well-groomed slave holdings
of Dawson's Plantation. And I was not
so naïve, upon hiring you, to believe
Dawson's high-minded economic philosophy
had not rubbed off on you.
But that's not what I called you for.
I bought a new buck yesterday:
here are his papers.

JONES

(Glancing through the documents.)

Miss Jennings! You can't be serious!

AMALIA

Something wrong, Jones?

JONES

Augustus Newcastle? That slave's
the most talked-about nigger
along the Southern seaboard!

AMALIA

Good! We'll be famous.

JONES   Story goes he belonged to a British sea captain
               who treated him like his own son,
               and promised him his freedom when he died.
               But the brother who executed the estate
               sold the boy to pay off the debts.
               After that, the nigger went wild.
               They lost count of how many times he ran off,
               how many times they caught him—

               Frantically leafs through the papers.

               here it is: "Twenty-two
               acts of aggression and rebellion."
               Twenty-two separate acts!

AMALIA   That's why I got him so cheaply.

JONES   But Miss Jennings! They say
               his back's so laced with scars
               it's as rutted as a country road.
               Rumor has it he can read and write.
               If you don't mind my saying so,
               Ma'am, an educated nigger
               brings nothing but trouble.
               Sure as I'm standing here,
               he'll stir up the others.

AMALIA   I wonder just how smart he is.

JONES   It's a miracle no one ever killed him.

AMALIA   (*Sharply.*)

               I own Augustus Newcastle,
               and I'll make him serve up.
               Any objections?

JONES   No, Ma'am. Sorry, Ma'am.

AMALIA   They're bringing him over tonight;
                   put him in the barn and chain him down.
                   You can show him around tomorrow.
                   If he's as smart as they say,
                   he could help you oversee the ginning.
                   You may go.

                   This last is a jab at JONES, who looks at her
                   for a moment, then turns on his heel and exits.

                   Blackout.

Scene 3

In the fields.

Sunday. The slaves have been "let out in the fields" to occupy themselves as they please. They have settled into two groups—some joke, tell stories, and dance, while others are quieter, chanting and praying. As the lights come up, the groups are rivaling each other in melody, the quieter ones humming in a minor key while the others counterpoint in a jauntier tune.

SCIPIO
Have you seen the new man?
Mister Jones been showing him around.

ALEXANDER
I saw 'em down
by the gin house.
That's one wild nigger.

PHEBE
He spent last night
chained in the barn.
Chained!

SCIPIO
Must be mighty tough.
Heard tell he's sailed the seas!

DIANA
Did he sail the seas to Canada?

Shocked silence; everybody looks at her.

ALEXANDER
Gal, don't let nobody
hear you say that word;
Miss Amalia'll have your head on a stick.
As far as you concerned
there's nothing in this world
but South Carolina and this here plantation.

AUGUSTUS enters in leg chains, followed by a watchful JONES. AUGUSTUS is a tall, handsome young man with caramel-toned skin and piercing eyes. His righteous anger is thinly concealed behind his slave mannerisms. JONES bluffs his way with a squeaky bravado.

JONES

Here's the new buck you all
been whispering about!

Removes the leg chains; then, to AUGUSTUS.

You're lucky it's Sunday. Tomorrow
you'll get a taste of how things run
around here. First horn at day-clean!

JONES exits. There is a moment's awkward silence as AUGUSTUS rubs his ankles where the chains have chafed. He looks up, calmly surveying the two groups.

SCIPIO

Welcome, stranger, welcome.
They call me Scipio.
What do you go by?

AUGUSTUS

Augustus.

SCIPIO

(*Stretching the name out, trying to make it fit his tongue.*)

Au-gus-tus?
Ain't never heard that one before.
What kind of name is that?

AUGUSTUS

The name of a king.

Uneasy silence.

PHEBE

Don't pay Scipio no mind.
He's always joking.
I'm Phebe. And this is Alexander.

ALEXANDER nods, warily.

Alexander been here longer than anyone, I reckon.

ALEXANDER

How do.

SCYLLA enters with a water gourd and watches the introductions with a hard eye. PHEBE rushes to introduce them.

PHEBE

And this here's Scylla. Scylla,
he's the new one, go by the name of—

AUGUSTUS

Augustus Newcastle.

SCYLLA

Newcastle. Is that your captain's name?

AUGUSTUS

Scylla was the rock,
Charybdis the whirlpool,
that pulled the sailors down.

General astonishment.

PHEBE

Now this little girl—

Pushes DIANA over to AUGUSTUS.

was born and raised
right here on this plantation.

AUGUSTUS	What's your name, child?
DIANA	(*Shyly.*)
	Diana.
AUGUSTUS	My, my. The sun and the moon all in one morning!

The SLAVES look bewildered. He laughs softly.

Don't mind me. I'm just glad to meet you all.

Some SLAVES take up their chant again. AUG-USTUS walks upstage and stands looking into the distance. Although they are curious, the other SLAVES let him be. Only DIANA stares after him.

PHEBE	Come on, Scipio, give us a story.
SCIPIO	You always wanting a story! How many stories you think I got?
PHEBE	I think you grow them in your sleep.
SCIPIO	Well, I ain't got a story this time.
PHEBE	Aw, Scipio! You dog!
SCIPIO	But I got a song:

Accompanies himself on a handmade string instru-ment while his friends clap, pat their bodies, etc.

The possum said, don't hurt me,
I'm harmless if you please!
The nigger said, I'm harmless, too,
And got down on his knees.

SCIPIO (con't.) The possum cocked his little head
And contemplated long;
You're running just like me, he said
And joined into the song.

Old Mr. Coon just happened by
Where the two sang merrily;
I don't trust you, cried Mr. Coon,
Why, you just as black as me!

You're just as black as me, Coon said,
but your tail ain't quite so long!
The Mr Coon ran in the woods
And wouldn't join their song.

Laughter. DIANA walks over to AUGUSTUS.

DIANA What you looking at?

AUGUSTUS Just looking.

DIANA Ain't nothing out there but the swamp.

AUGUSTUS Do you know what's beyond that swamp?

DIANA What?

AUGUSTUS The world.

PHEBE (*To SCIPIO.*)

Is that all?

SCIPIO No, there's more:

Singing.

The nigger wrapped his fingers
Around the possum's throat.
The possum didn't have the time
To sing another note.

That night the nigger had himself
A pot of possum stew.
That harmless meat is just the thing
To warm your innards through!

DIANA   What did you mean by
the sun and the moon?

AUGUSTUS   Beg pardon?

DIANA   The sun and the moon—you asked
my name and then you said you had
the sun and the moon all in one day.

AUGUSTUS   You're a curious one, aren't you?

DIANA   Uh-huh.

AUGUSTUS   Well—a long time ago there were
gods to look after the earth and the sky.
Phoebus was the god of the sun;
your friend's name is Phebe.
And your name stood for the moon.
People wrote poems to Diana,
goddess of the moon.

DIANA   What's poems?

AUGUSTUS   A poem is...

Looking over at SCIPIO.

AUGUSTUS (con't.)   ...a song without music.

Looks off towards the swamp.

Who's that old man?

DIANA   Phebe, Hector's coming up from the swamp!

PHEBE   Don't fret, chile.
Hector talk kind of crazy sometimes,
but he don't hurt nobody.

AUGUSTUS   His name is Hector?

PHEBE   Yeah. Massa Jennings give it to him
straight off the boat. He used to talk
African—but he forgot most of it.

AUGUSTUS   What does he do in the swamp?

PHEBE   (*Catching a warning look from SCYLLA.*)

He lives there.

AUGUSTUS   Hector, mighty warrior,
abandoned by the gods.

DIANA   You know a lot of things.

AUGUSTUS   Nothing you couldn't learn
if you had the chance.

*Enter HECTOR, now middle-aged, dressed in
muddy rags. He carries a dead snake in a net and
looks around with wild, piercing eyes, then wanders
up to DIANA.*

HECTOR	(*Tenderly.*)
	Eshu Elewa ogo gbogbo!
	DIANA shrinks back. HECTOR taps AUGUSTUS on the shoulder, holding out the net.
	I catch snakes: big ones, little ones. I'm going to catch all the snakes in the swamp.
AUGUSTUS	I don't know much about snakes, my friend.
HECTOR	I'm gonna catch all the snakes in the swamp! They grow and grow, so many of them. But I'll kill them! I'll kill them all!
SCYLLA	Shh, Hector! Don't let the snakes hear!
	She puts her arm around HECTOR and pats him gently on the back, all the while staring at AUGUSTUS, as the lights dim and go out.

Scene 4

SCYLLA's cabin and the area outside of the slave cabins.

Night. SCYLLA sits in her cabin behind a crude table strewn with an assortment of bones, twisted roots, beads, and dried corncobs. Three candles light up her face from below. AUGUSTUS, in ankle chains, squats outside the slave cabins. In the distance can be heard the rhythmic ecstasy of the Sunday night "shout". PHEBE at the door with a small cloth bundle. She looks behind her.

SCYLLA   Come in, child. Sit.

                   PHEBE sits.

                   I know your heart, Phebe.
                   You have made the spirits angry!

PHEBE   I never meant no harm—

SCYLLA   Shh!

                   Picks out a forked branch and arranges the candles in a half-circle around the branch.

                   The body moves through the world.

                   Places a round white stone in the fork of the branch.

                   The mind rests in the body.

                   Sprinkles green powder from a vial onto branch and stone.

The soul is bright
as a jewel, lighter than air.

Blows the powder away; the candles flare,
PHEBE coughs.

There is a curse on the land.
The net draws closer.
What have you brought?

PHEBE   Here!

Shoves her bundle across the table. SCYLLA
pulls out a pink ribbon and drapes it over the
branch.

SCYLLA   "Eshu Elewa ogo gbogbo...

Sprinkling powder on the first candle.

...oki kosi eyo!"

The candle flares and goes out.

You have tried to make the earth
give up her dead.

PHEBE   Oh!

SCYLLA   (*Pulling out a shell necklace, draping it over the*
branch.)

"Kosi eyo,
kosi iku...

Sprinkling powder on the second candle.

...kosi ano!"

The second candle goes out.

PHEBE   Have mercy...

SCYLLA   You have tried to snatch words
                 back from the air. The wind is angry.
                 It will take more than these—

                 Indicating PHEBE's offerings.

                 to satisfy him.

PHEBE   *(Pulls a white handkerchief out of her pocket.)*

                 Here's...a hankie from my mama.
                 There's a little lace on it—see?

                 *SCYLLA snatches the handkerchief, places it on
                 the branch and repeats the procedure with pow-
                 der and incantation.*

SCYLLA   "Ni oru ko mi gbogbo
                 omonile fu kuikuo
                 modupue—
                 baba mi Elewa!"

                 The third candle flickers but stays lit.

                 Ah!

PHEBE   What is it?

SCYLLA   Are you prepared to hear
                 what the spirits have to say?

PHEBE   *(Gathering courage.)*

                 If there's something I need to know,
                 I want to know it.

SCYLLA	I give you two warnings. One: guard your footsteps; they are your mark on the earth. If a sharp stone or piece of glass falls into the path you have walked, you will go lame. Two: guard your breath; do not throw with words. Whenever the wind blows, if your mouth is open, your soul could be snatched away. That is all.
PHEBE	Scylla...
SCYLLA	Go now!

SCYLLA mutters over the candles as PHEBE hurries off, shuffling her feet to blur her footprints as she flees. On the way she passes AUGUSTUS. In the distance the SLAVES can be heard humming during the "shout".

AUGUSTUS	Evening.
PHEBE	(*Caught in the act of obliterating her steps; embarrassed.*) Evening.
AUGUSTUS	Back from the shout?
PHEBE	(*Trying not to speak.*) Uh-uh.
AUGUSTUS	What's your hurry? Why don't you keep me company for a spell? Unless you're scared of me, that is.

PHEBE   Scared of you? Why should
                         I be scared of you?

AUGUSTUS   I can't think of a reason in the world.
                         Come on, rest yourself.

                         PHEBE sits down beside him carefully.

AUGUSTUS   Sure is a fine night.

                         PHEBE nods.

                         You're trembling.

PHEBE   I am?

                         Claps her hand over her mouth.

AUGUSTUS   And I don't believe
                         it's entirely my doing.

                         *He says this in a mildly flirtatious manner, then
                         looks off, unaware of the effect this has on PHEBE,
                         who has stopped thinking about SCYLLA and is
                         now acutely aware of AUGUSTUS as a man.
                         AUGUSTUS continues speaking, preoccupied
                         once again with his hatred.*

                         Fear! Fear eats out the heart.
                         It'll cause kings and field niggers alike
                         to crawl in their own piss. Listen
                         to them sing!
                         What kind of god preaches such misery?

                         Gesturing in the direction of the "shout".

                         White-fearing niggers.
                         Death-fearing slaves.

PHEBE	Ain't you ever scared?
AUGUSTUS	Of what? White folks? They're more afraid of me. Pain? Every whipping's got to come to an end.
PHEBE	I heard you've been whipped so many times, they lost count.
AUGUSTUS	They think they can beat me to my senses. Then they look into my eyes and see I'm not afraid.
PHEBE	It'd be something, not to be afraid.
AUGUSTUS	You have to have a purpose. Something bigger than anything they can do to you.
PHEBE	(*Suppressing a shudder.*) And ain't nobody ever tried to kill you?
AUGUSTUS	Oh, yes. First time, I was hardly alive. They ripped me from my mother the night I was born and threw me out like trash. I didn't walk until I was three.
PHEBE	Lord have mercy.
AUGUSTUS	Mercy had nothing to do with it! Missy couldn't stand the sight of me. Just look at me! It's an old story. You've stopped trembling. Now why don't you tell me what made you quake that way in the first place?

PHEBE shakes her head.

Conjuration, I imagine?
Mumble-jumble from that hateful woman.

PHEBE   Her name's Scylla.

AUGUSTUS   Women like her, hah!
                  They get a chill one morning,
                  hear an owl or two, and snap!—
                  they've received their "powers"!
                  Then they collect a few old bones,
                  dry some herbs, and they're in business.

PHEBE   She told me to watch my footsteps—

AUGUSTUS   —or you'd fall lame.

PHEBE   And to keep my mouth shut
                  when the wind blowed—

AUGUSTUS   —or else the wind spirit
                  would steal your soul.

PHEBE   How'd you know?

AUGUSTUS   You think she's the only conjure-woman
                  in the world? Why, your Scylla's a baby
                  compared to the voodoo chiefs in the islands.
                  They can kill you with a puff of smoke
                  from their pipes—if you believe in them.
                  Take me: I've been cursed enough times
                  to bring down a whole fleet of ships
                  around me—but here I sit, high and dry.
                  So I guess they must be saving me
                  for something special.

PHEBE looks at AUGUSTUS in wonder; the lights dim as the other SLAVES slowly come on stage, singing as they take their places in the fields. The song sung during the "shout" has modulated into a percussive piece with no words—clapping, sighs, whispered exclamations and grunts punctuate what becomes a work song.

SLAVES

No way out, gotta keep on—
No way but to see it through.

NARRATOR

Don't sass, don't fight!
Lay low, grin bright!

NARRATOR/
SLAVES

No way but to see it through.

Scene 5

The cotton fields. The light brightens: high noon. JONES enters, looks at the sun and cracks his whip as he calls out.

JONES   Noon!

He exits, wiping his brow with a huge handkerchief. The SLAVES groan and sigh as they settle down with their provisions—cornpone and salt pork and gourds of water.

ALEXANDER   *(Making sure that JONES is out of earshot.)*

I swear on all my years
there's nothing I hate so much as cotton.
Picking, toting, weighing, tramping:
the work keeps coming.

SCIPIO   No end in sight, and that's the truth!

Leans back, hands under head.

Now what I'd fancy is a life at sea.
Sun and sky and blue water,
with just a sip of rum
every once in a while.
You been to sea, Augustus.
What's it like?

AUGUSTUS   It ain't the easy life.

SCIPIO   But what's it like, man?
The closest I been to the sea
was when the cotton gin came in

to Charleston port. All those fine
flapping sails and tall masts,
cotton bales stacked to heaven...
Did you visit lots of strange places?

AUGUSTUS   We sailed the West Indies route.
Stocked up rum, tobacco, beads—

SCYLLA   (*Scathingly.*)

—and traded them for slaves.
Did you have to ride cargo?

AUGUSTUS   (*With a sharp look, sarcastically.*)

Cap'n Newcastle was a generous master.

Resuming his story.

But those ports! Sand so white,
from far off it looked like
spilled cream. Palm trees taller
than our masts, loaded with coconuts.

DIANA   What's a coconut?

AUGUSTUS   It's a big brown gourd
with hair on it like a dog,
and when you break it open
sweet milk pours out.

DIANA   What does it taste like?

AUGUSTUS   It tastes like...
just coconut. There's nothing like it.

SCYLLA   Your stories stir up trouble,
young man.

PHEBE moves as if to stop him; he motions her back.

AUGUSTUS
Seems you're the only one
who's riled up, Scylla.

SCYLLA
You're what we call an uppity nigger.
And uppity niggers always trip themselves up.

AUGUSTUS
Are you going to put a curse on me, too,
Scylla? Cross your eyes
and wave a few roots in the air
until I fall on my knees?

SCYLLA
No need to curse you;
you have been cursed already.

AUGUSTUS
You feed on ignorance
and call it magic. What kind of prophet
works against her own people?

The SLAVES murmur. SCYLLA stands up.

SCYLLA
Oh, you may dance now,
but you will fall.
The evil inside you
will cut you down to your knees,
and you will crawl—crawl in front of us all!

*Lights dim, then grow mottled and swamp-green as
all exit.*

Scene 6

The swamp. Lights remain mottled and swamp-green. Night sounds filter in as HECTOR enters.

HECTOR   Easy, easy: don't tell the cook
the meat's gone bad.

Slashes at the underbrush.

We got to cut it out.
Ya! Ya!

Hacks in rhythm for a moment.

I can smell it. Pah!

Sniffs, then peers.

But there's a rose in the gravy, oh yes—
a rose shining through the mists, a red smell.
Red and mean.

But how sweet she smelled!
Cottons and flowers.
And lemons that bite back
when you touch them to the tongue.

Shh! Don't tell the cook.
Black folks fiddle, the white folks stare.

*There is a bird call; HECTOR conceals himself.
AUGUSTUS enters; he appears to be following the
sound. He gives out a matching call, then bursts into
a clearing in the swamp where a group of black men
sit in a circle around a small fire, chanting softly. The
LEADER of the group rises.*

LEADER   There you are!
                  We've called two nights.

AUGUSTUS   Who are you?

LEADER   Patience, Augustus Newcastle.
                  Oh yes, we know all about you.

AUGUSTUS   What do you want?

LEADER   Your courage has been a beacon—

CONSPIRATORS   Amen! Selah!

                  The CONSPIRATORS surround the LEADER;
                  they react to his words in a call-and-response fash-
                  ion; their movements are vaguely ritualistic and
                  creepy, as if they were under a spell; this effect can
                  be enhanced with dance and pantomime. AUG-
                  USTUS stands still as the CONSPIRATORS
                  swarm around him, occasionally trying to pull him
                  among them.

LEADER   — and we need men willing to fight
                  for freedom! Tell me, Augustus Newcastle:
                  are you prepared to sign your name
                  with the revolutionary forces?

AUGUSTUS   First tell me who you are.

LEADER   So cautious? We expected a bit more daring
                  from someone of your reputation.

AUGUSTUS   I am many things, but I'm not a fool.

LEADER   (*Laughs.*)

                  Shall we show him, brothers?

CONSPIRATORS	Selah!
LEADER	Each of us has been called forth as a warrior of righteousness. Each wandered in darkness until he found the light of brotherhood! Take young Benjamin Skeene:

BENJAMIN squares his shoulders as he steps for-
ward; he is a trim young man who, judging from
his clothes, must be either a house slave or a free-
man.

	As a skilled carpenter, he enjoys a fair amount of freedom.
BENJAMIN	The boss man's glad I can make his deliveries.
LEADER	So we've arranged a few deposits of our own. Benjamin, can you find a way to fasten this blade to a pole?
BENJAMIN	Easy.
LEADER	Every man who can wield a stick shall have a bayonet!
CONSPIRATORS	Selah!
LEADER	A few were more reluctant... or shall I say cautious? Henry Blake, for instance:

HENRY, a dark, middle-aged man, steps forward
hesitantly.

LEADER (con't.)	Fear had made him grateful for every crumb his master dropped him.
	The two act out the following exchange.
HENRY	I don't want no part of this!
LEADER	You followed the sign; you have been called!
HENRY	Any fool knows a mockingbird when he hears one—and that weren't no mockingbird!
LEADER	(*Threatening.*) Are you prepared to slay our oppressors, male and female, when it is deemed time, according to the plans of insurrection drawn up and approved by members present?
HENRY	I'm against the white man much as all of you—but murder? "Thou shalt not kill," saith the Commandments.
LEADER	Who made your master?
HENRY	God.
LEADER	And who made you?
HENRY	God.
LEADER	Then aren't you as good as your master if God made you both?

HENRY	I'm not a vengeful man.
LEADER	But our Lord is a vengeful God. "Whoever steals a man," He says, "whether he sells him or is found in possession of him, shall be put to death." Who is not with us is against us. You answered the call. If you turn back now...

HENRY slowly lifts his head, squares his shoulders, and remains frozen in the spotlight while the LEADER speaks to AUGUSTUS.

LEADER	He was brought to reason.
CONSPIRATORS	Selah.
LEADER	So the one becomes many and the many, one. Hence our password: "May Fate be with you—
CONSPIRATORS	And with us all!"
AUGUSTUS	Now I see who you are.
LEADER	Augustus Newcastle: are you prepared to slay our oppressors, male and female, when it is deemed time, according to the plans of insurrection drawn up and approved by members present?

AUGUSTUS	I am.
LEADER	Enter your name in the Book of Redemption!

AUGUSTUS signs the book.

CONSPIRATORS	Selah! Selah!
AUGUSTUS	Tell me what to do.
LEADER	You'll need a second-in-command. Report your choice to us; we will send out the sign.

Turning to the group.

My brothers, it is time to be free!
Maps are being prepared
of the city and its surroundings
along with the chief points of attack.
Bullets wait in kegs under the dock.
Destiny calls!

CONSPIRATORS	Amen!
LEADER	There are barrels of gun powder stacked in a cave outside Dawson's Plantation. Our Toby has been busy—

CONSPIRATORS nod and laugh in consent.

but he cannot risk further expeditions.
Henry Blake!

HENRY steps forward.

Your owner praised you in the marketplace
as the most trustworthy nigger

he ever had the fortune of owning.
Now it is up to you
to put your master's trust to the test.

HENRY bows his head in assent, steps back into the group.

Destiny calls us! The reckoning is nigh!
But remember: trust no-one.
All those who are not with us
are against us, blacks as well
as whites. Oh, do not falter!
Bolster your heart with the memory
of the atrocities committed upon your mothers.
Gird your loins with vengeance,
strap on the shining sword of freedom!

CONSPIRATORS   Selah!

LEADER   Brothers, are you with me?

CONSPIRATORS   Right behind you!

LEADER   Then nothing can stop us now!

AUGUSTUS   (*Blurting out.*)

                My orders! What are my orders?

LEADER   (*A little taken aback, but decides on the role of the amused patriarch.*)

                Patience, my son! Patience and cunning.
                Sow discontent among your brethren,
                inspire them to fury.

AUGUSTUS   I can do more. Read maps, write passes—

LEADER	That is all for now. Is that clear?
	Strained silence; the LEADER speaks reassur- *ingly.*
	You will recognize the signal.
	The CONSPIRATORS begin humming "Steal *Away".*
LEADER	Go to your people and test their minds; so when the fires of redemption lick the skies of Charleston, they will rise up, up— a mighty army marching into battle!
CONSPIRATORS	Steal away, steal away, Steal away to Jesus! Steal away, steal away home, I ain't got long to stay here.
	The CONSPIRATORS continue singing as *they exchange farewells and slip off. HECTOR* *appears at the edge of the undergrowth, a dead* *snake in his outstretched arms.*
	Blackout.

Scene 7

The cotton fields.

NARRATOR

A sniff of freedom's all it takes
to feel history's sting;
there's danger by-and-by
when the slaves won't sing.

*JONES supervises the picking, which transpires
without singing; the silence is eerie. JONES' appear-
ance is slovenly, as if he's already been drinking.*

JONES

Move it, nigger! Faster!
What you glaring at? Faster!

*The SLAVES continue picking at the same rate.
JONES looks at the sun, then cracks his whip.*

Aw, the hell with ya! Noon!

*He stumbles offstage. The SLAVES divide into two
groups: some hum spirituals while the others gather
around AUGUSTUS.*

SCIPIO

Come on, Augustus, what else?

AUGUSTUS

Did you know there are slaves
who have set themselves free?

SCIPIO

(*Almost afraid to ask.*)

How'd they do that?

AUGUSTUS	Santo Domingo, San Domingue, Hispaniola— three names for an island rising like a fortress from the waters of the Caribbean. An island of sun and forest, wild fruit and mosquitoes— and slaves, many slaves—half a million. Slaves to chop sugar, slaves to pick coffee beans, slaves to do their French masters' every bidding.

AUGUSTUS

Santo Domingo, San Domingue, Hispaniola—
three names for an island
rising like a fortress
from the waters of the Caribbean.
An island of sun and forest,
wild fruit and mosquitoes—
and slaves, many slaves—half a million.
Slaves to chop sugar, slaves
to pick coffee beans, slaves to do
their French masters' every bidding.

Then one summer, news came
from the old country: Revolution!
Plantation owners broke into a sweat;
their slaves served cool drinks
while the masters rocked on their verandas,
discussing each outrage:
people marching against the king,
crowds pouring into the streets,
shouting three words:
Liberté!

SLAVES

We shall be free!

AUGUSTUS

Égalité!

SLAVES

Master and slave.

AUGUSTUS

Fraternité!

SLAVES

Brothers and sisters!

AUGUSTUS

Liberté, Égalité, Fraternité—three words
were all the island masters talked about
that summer, while their slaves
served carefully and listened.

SLAVES

Liberté, Égalité, Fraternité!

During the following speech, a smouldering growl
among the SLAVES grows louder and louder, until
it explodes in a shout.

AUGUSTUS

Black men meeting in the forest:
Eight days, they whispered,
and we'll be free. For eight days
bonfires flashed in the hills:
Equality. For eight days
tom-toms spoke in the mountains:
Liberty. For eight days
the tom-toms sang: Brothers and sisters.
And on the eighth day, swift as lightning,
the slaves attacked.

SLAVES

Yah!

AMALIA enters, unseen, and stands listening.

AUGUSTUS

They came down the mountains
to the sound of tambourines and conch shells.
With torches they swept onto the plantations,
with the long harvest knives
they chopped white men down
like sugar cane. For three weeks
the flames raged; then the sun
broke through the smoke and shone
upon a new nation, a black nation—
Haiti!

SLAVES

Haiti!

AUGUSTUS

(*Looking intently at the faces around him.*)

Now do you see
why they've kept this from us,
brothers and sisters?

AMALIA	A lovely speech.
	The SLAVES are horrified. AUGUSTUS stands impassive.
	I see you're a poet as well as a rebel.
	JONES rushes in.
JONES	Anything wrong, Miss Jennings?
AMALIA	Not a thing, Jones. Just passing the time of day with my happy flock— which is more than I see you doing.
JONES	But it's noon, Miss Jennings! They need nourishment if we're going to get this crop in.
AMALIA	It appears they've been getting a different sort of sustenance.
JONES	*(Uncomprehending.)* Beg pardon, Ma'am?
AMALIA	*(Impatient with JONES.)* See that they work an extra hour tonight. I don't care if they have to pick by moonlight! *To AUGUSTUS.* As for you: I'll see you up at the house. Come at sunset— the view over the fields is most enchanting then. *She strides off. Blackout.*

Scene 8

The big house, LOUIS' study and the parlor.

Twilight filters through the curtains; the frogs have started up in the swamp.

LOUIS paces back and forth in his room, holding a chart; he stops to stare at it for a moment, then waves it in disgust and paces once more.

LOUIS　　　　　　Something's out there: I can feel it!
　　　　　　　　What a discovery it would be.
　　　　　　　　But no—

　　　　　　　　Grabs his brandy.

　　　　　　　　No new coin shines
　　　　　　　　for Louis LaFarge
　　　　　　　　among the stars!

　　　　　　　　He stops at the window and stares out.

　　　　　　　　AMALIA sits in the parlor reading, a decanter of sherry and a tea service on the table next to the sofa. The evening song of the SLAVES floats in from the fields—a plaintive air with a compelling affirmation of life, a strange melody with no distinct beat or tune. TICEY, the old house slave, enters.

TICEY　　　　　　Miss Amalia?

AMALIA　　　　　*(Without turning.)*

　　　　　　　　Yes?

TICEY　　　　　　That new slave, Ma'am—
　　　　　　　　he's standing at the front porch!

AMALIA   (*Amused.*)

                  The front porch? Well, show him in, Ticey!

                  *TICEY exits; AMALIA rises and goes to the win-
                  dow. She is looking out toward the fields when
                  AUGUSTUS appears in the doorway. Although
                  she knows he is there, she does not turn around.*

AMALIA   What are they singing?

AUGUSTUS   No words you'd understand.
                  No tune you'd recognise.

AMALIA   And how is it they all sing together?

AUGUSTUS   It's the sorrow songs.
                  They don't need a psalm book.

AMALIA   (*Resumes her imperious manner.*)

                  "Personal servant to Captain Newcastle
                  of the schooner Victoria. Ports of call:
                  St Thomas, Tobago, St Croix,
                  Martinique"—in other words,
                  a slave ship.

AUGUSTUS   Yes.

AMALIA   And what did you learn
                  under your captain's tutelage?

AUGUSTUS   Reading. Writing. Figures.

AMALIA   What did you read?

AUGUSTUS   Milton. The Bible.
                  And the Tales of the Greeks.

AMALIA   (*Thrusting the book she's been reading at him.*)

                See the blue ribbon sticking out?
                You may start there.

                AUGUSTUS turns the book over to read the title,
                then looks at her for a moment before returning it.
                She snatches the book.

AMALIA   Too difficult? No doubt you'd do better
                with the Greek original—

                Slyly.

                but we are not that cultured a household.

                Circling him.

                I wondered could there be a nigger alive
                smart as this one's claimed to be?
                Of course, if there were, he might
                be smart enough to pretend
                he wasn't smart at all.

AUGUSTUS   No pretense. I've read that one already.
                In my opinion, the Greeks
                were a bit too predictable.

AMALIA   A slave has no opinion!

                Regaining her composure.

                I could have you flogged to your bones
                for what you did today.

AUGUSTUS   Why didn't you?

                The SLAVES stop singing.

AMALIA   Daddy said a master knows his slaves
              better than they know themselves.
              And he never flogged a slave—
              he said it was a poor businessman
              who damaged his own merchandise.

AUGUSTUS   (*Sarcastically.*)

              An enlightened man, your father.

AMALIA   He let me run wild until
              it was time to put on crinolines.
              My playmates were sent to the fields,
              and I was sent to the parlor with needlework—
              a scented, dutiful daughter.

AUGUSTUS   Most men find intelligence troubling
              in a woman—even fathers.

AMALIA   Then, off I went to finishing school: Miss Peeters'
              Academy for Elocution and Deportment!
              "The art of conversation," she used to say—
              please, sit down!—"is to make
              the passing of time agreeable."

              Arranging her dress as she sits on the sofa.

              "suitable subjects are—"
              Sit down, I said!

              Softer, but with an edge.

              One does not conduct conversation
              while standing.

              *She indicates a chair, upholstered in champagne-colored
              tufted damask. AUGUSTUS moves toward it but swiftly
              and gracefully drops cross-legged to the floor, daringly close
              to AMALIA's slippered feet. She starts to pull away—
              then slowly extends her feet again.*

"Suitable subjects for
genteel conversation are:

Ticking them off on her fingers.

"Nature. Travel. History.
And above all, culture—
painting, music, and books."

We'll, we're done with books!
Tell me, Mr Newcastle—
was the weather in the Indies
very different from here?

AUGUSTUS   Warmer.

AMALIA   Is that all?

AUGUSTUS   There was always a breeze.

AMALIA   And an abundance of exotic
                foods, I'm sure.

AUGUSTUS   We had our share of papaya.

                *The SLAVES start up a new song, more
                African in rhythm and harmonies.*

AMALIA   Imagine that. Subject number two:
                Travel. So many ports!

                Shaking her head charmingly.

                Did Captain Newcastle
                allow you to go ashore
                at St Thomas, Tobago, Martinique?

AUGUSTUS   (*On guard.*)

                No.

AMALIA   Charleston has welcomed a fair share
              of immigrants to her shores.

              Laughs delicately.

              There was that Haiti business around the time
              I was born. Over five hundred French plantation owners
              fled here. The whole city was in panic.
              Why, my dear husband—hear him pacing
              up there, wearing out the floorboards?—
              little Louis showed up in Charleston harbor
              that year, with his blue blood *maman* and *papa.*
              Liberté, Égalité, Fraternité!

              Looking directly at AUGUSTUS.

              It was a brilliant revolution.
              I've often wondered why our niggers
              don't revolt. I've said to myself:
              "Amalia, if you had been a slave,
              you most certainly would have plotted
              an insurrection by now."

              Turns away from AUGUSTUS.

              But we say all sorts of things
              to ourselves, don't we?
              There's no telling what we'd do
              if the moment were there for the taking.

              Lights up on LOUIS, still staring out the window.

LOUIS   You can't hide forever.
              There's a hole in the heavens,
              and you're throbbing right behind it.

              Whispers.

              I can feel you.

AMALIA	Have you ever heard of the *Amistad*?
AUGUSTUS	Why?
AMALIA	The *Amistad*: a slave ship. Three days off the port of Principe the Africans freed themselves and attacked with machetes and harpoons. Cinque, their leader, spared two sailors to steer them back to Africa. But Cinque was unfamiliar with the stars in our hemisphere. Each morning he set course east by the sun; each night the sailors turned the ship and steered west—until they managed to land on our coast and deliver Cinque and his followers to execution.
AUGUSTUS	A bit of a storybook ending, isn't it?
AMALIA	What's that supposed to mean?
AUGUSTUS	It's just so perfect a lesson.
AMALIA	You don't believe me? It was in the newspapers. *Significantly.* You followed your precious captain everywhere; you were there when he loaded slave cargo into the hold or plotted a new course. What an admirable science, navigation! It must be terribly complicated, even for you.

AUGUSTUS *(Getting up from the floor.)*

Now I have a story for you.
Once there was a preacher slave
went by the name of Isaac.
When God called him
he was a boy, out hunting rice birds.
Killing rice birds is easy—
just pinch off their heads.

Indicating the sherry.

May I?

AMALIA flinches, nods. He pours the sherry expertly.

But one day, halfway up the tree
where a nest of babies chirped,
a voice called out: "Don't do it, Isaac."
It was an angel, shining
in the crook of a branch.
Massa let him preach.
What harm could it do?

Sitting down in the damask chair.

Then a slave uprising in Virginia
had all the white folks
watching their own niggers
for signs of treachery.
No more prayer meetings, Isaac!
But God would not wait,
so Isaac kept on preaching
at night, in the woods.

Of course he was caught.
Three of his congregation
were shot on the spot, three others branded

and their feet pierced.
But what to do about Isaac,
gentle Isaac who had turned traitor?

AMALIA　　　　　Is there a point to this?

AUGUSTUS　　　　I'm just passing the time of evening
with...conversation.

*Upstairs, LOUIS positions his telescope at the
window and searches the heavens.*

LOUIS　　　　　There it is...no, wait!
Gone.

Shakes his head in despair.

Sometimes I catch
a glimmer, a hot blue flash—
then it disappears.
Show yourself, demon!

*In the parlor, AUGUSTUS takes a sip of sherry
and continues.*

AUGUSTUS　　　　First they flogged him. Then
they pickled the wounds with salt water,
and when they were nearly healed,
he was flogged again, and the wounds
pickled again, and on and on for weeks
while Massa sold off Isaac's children
one by one. They took him to see
his wife on the auction block,
baby at her breast.
A week later it was his turn.
His back had finally healed;
but as his new owner led him
from the auction block,
Isaac dropped down dead.

AUGUSTUS (con't.)   *Pause; more to himself than to AMALIA.*

They couldn't break his spirit,
so they broke his heart.

*They stare at each other for a moment; then
AMALIA rises and walks to the window. It has
gotten dark outside.*

AMALIA   They're still singing.
How can they have songs left?

AUGUSTUS   *(Joining her at the window.)*

As many songs as sorrows.

AMALIA   And you, Augustus? Were you ever happy?

AUGUSTUS   Happy? No.

AMALIA   Never? Not even on the ship
with the whole sea around you?

AUGUSTUS   I was a boy. I felt lucky, not happy.

AMALIA   I was happy once.
I traded it for luck.

AUGUSTUS   Luck's a dangerous master.

AMALIA   Half my life I spent dreaming,
the other half burying dreams.

Bitter laugh, turns to AUGUSTUS.

Funny, isn't it?

AUGUSTUS   (*Turns away from her with difficulty, stares out the
                    window.*)

                    One soft spring night
                    when the pear blossoms
                    cast their pale faces
                    on the darker face of the earth,
                    Massa stood up from the porch swing
                    and said to himself, "I think
                    I'll make me another bright-eyed pickaninny."
                    Then he stretched and headed
                    for my mother's cabin. And now—
                    that pickaninny, who started out
                    no more than the twinkle in a white man's eye
                    and the shame between his mama's legs—
                    now he stands in the parlor of
                    another massa, entertaining the pretty mistress
                    with stories of whippings and heartbreak.

AMALIA   (*Half to herself.*)

                    Pretty? Am I pretty?

AUGUSTUS   (*Answers in spite of himself.*)

                    You can put a rose in a vase
                    with a bunch of other flowers;
                    but when you walk into the room
                    the rose is the only thing you see.

                    *AMALIA touches his wrist, then traces the vein up
                    his arm, as if remembering.*

AMALIA   Imagine! A life without even
                    a smidgen of happiness...

AUGUSTUS   (*Wrestling with desire.*)

                    I'm not one of your dreams.

AMALIA   No? Perhaps not. What a pity.

She touches his cheek; he holds her hand there.
They lean towards each other slowly, as the
SLAVES' sorrow song surges—but before their
lips touch, there is a blackout.

ACT TWO

Scene 1

Dream sequence.

Dimly lit, the light rather blue. Each group is in its appointed "place" on stage—AMALIA in her parlour with TICEY standing impassively in the background; LOUIS above, in his study; most SLAVES going about their chores; SCYLLA isolated, with her herbs and potions. In the swamp, HECTOR searches for snakes; the CONSPIRATORS huddle, occasionally lifting a fist into the circle. AUGUSTUS stands front and centre, back to the audience, gazing at AMALIA. Mostly silhouettes are seen, except when a single voice rises out of the chanting, which will grow to cacophony at the end of the sequence.

SLAVES
They have bowed our heads,
they have bent our backs.
Mercy, mercy,
Lord above, mercy.

AMALIA
I slept, but my heart was awake.
How beautiful he is!

SLAVES
Lord have mercy.
They have bowed our heads...

SCYLLA
There's a curse on the land.
The net draws closer.

HECTOR
Under rocks, 'twixt reeds and roots...

SLAVES
They have bent our backs,
they have snatched our songs...

AUGUSTUS	(*Singing.*)
	Sometimes I feel like a motherless child...
SLAVES	(*Joining in.*)
	A motherless child, a motherless child, sometimes I feel like a motherless child—
	Continue humming through most of the scene.
LOUIS	(*In a scientific voice, detached, as if reciting.*)
	Every night at the same hour, each star appears slightly to the west of its previous position. Scientists calculate that the 12 houses of the zodiac have shifted so radically since ancient times, their relation to each other may now signify completely different portents.
HECTOR	So many, so many.
SLAVES	(*Singing.*)
	A long way from home.
AUGUSTUS	One soft night, Massa stood up—
CONSPIRATORS	Selah.
AUGUSTUS	— and laughed to himself.
CONSPIRATORS	It is time.
SCYLLA	The net draws tighter.
CONSPIRATORS	Selah!

AUGUSTUS	One darkening evening, I stood up—
	SLAVES humming, CONSPIRATORS chanting "Selah" in a barely audible whisper.
	— and she was mine, mine all night, until the day breathed fire and the shadows fled.
AMALIA	Look, how beautiful he is!
CONSPIRATORS	Rise up!
SLAVES	(*Simultaneously.*)
	Mercy, mercy.
AMALIA	His eyes, his brow, his cheeks—
CONSPIRATORS	Rise up!
AMALIA	— his lips...
AUGUSTUS	...until the day breathed fire...
HECTOR	Eshu Elewa...ogo...gbogbo.
SLAVES	They have bowed our heads, they have bent our backs.
SCYLLA	Closer...
	PHEBE dashes to center-stage, hands outstretched as if to hold back a flood.
PHEBE	Stop it! Stop!!!
	Everyone freezes.

Scene 2

The tableau remains.

PHEBE drops her arms and moves slightly stage-left. AUGUSTUS, with his back still to the audience, backs downstage, towards the slave cabins, looking alternately at AMALIA and the CONSPIRATORS until the tableau disintegrates. PHEBE taps him on the shoulder, and he whirls around.

PHEBE	Evenin'.
AUGUSTUS	Oh! Phebe. Evening.
PHEBE	You're trembling.
AUGUSTUS	I am?
	Laughs.
	Cold spell coming on, I imagine.
PHEBE	No, that's what you said to me!
	AUGUSTUS looks at her, uncomprehending.
	That time I was coming back from Scylla's, scared to open my mouth, you said: "What's your hurry?" And then you said, "You're trembling," and I said, "I am?" —just like you did now.
AUGUSTUS	Oh.
PHEBE	What's your hurry? Heading up to the House again?

AUGUSTUS   I got a moment.

PHEBE   Sit yourself down, then.
               Rest a spell.

               They sit side by side; PHEBE embarrassed,
               AUGUSTUS nervous.

PHEBE   You sure be up there a long time.
               At the Big House, I mean.

AUGUSTUS   (*Tersely.*)

               Missy's orders.

PHEBE   What else she have you doing?

AUGUSTUS   We practice the fine art of conversation.

PHEBE   Quit fooling!

AUGUSTUS   Oh, yes, we talk about everything—
               weather and the science of navigation,
               recent history and ancient literature.

PHEBE   What's that she-fox up to now?

AUGUSTUS   It's simple: she wants to tame me.
               And if I get better treatment
               than the rest of you,
               all my talk about Haiti
               won't hold much water.

PHEBE   So she think she can get us
               to fighting amongst ourselves!

AUGUSTUS   Seems plenty folks want things
               just the way they are.
               Alexander keeps his distance, lately.

93

PHEBE	Alexander's seen his share of sorrow. He just wants to live in peace.
AUGUSTUS	And die in peace?
PHEBE	(*Not catching his drift.*)

I 'spect so. Who doesn't?
Oh, that's right—
you and Death gonna walk outta here
hand and hand!

PHEBE laughs; AUGUSTUS is spooked.

Alexander don't mean you no spite.
And Scipio—Scipio say
you his man, any time, any place!
You shoulda seen him the other day,
putting voodoo spells on the chickens!
Then he pick up the milk bucket
and pranced around, serving up
revolution lemonade! Now there's
a body need of some occupation!

AUGUSTUS	(*Aside.*)

Maybe I can help him find it.

PHEBE	'Course, you got Diana's heart. She thinks the sun and the moon set in your face.
AUGUSTUS	Then there's Scylla.
PHEBE	Hmmpf! Woman had me nearly crazy, clamping my mouth and wiping my footsteps so I ended up getting nowhere.

As far as I'm concerned,
Scylla can roll her eye and talk conjuration
till the summer go cold and the cotton pick itself!

AUGUSTUS   Now, that's the fire I saw!

PHEBE   Huh?

AUGUSTUS   The first time I saw you,
I thought to myself:
"That's not the spirit of a slave.
That's a pure flame."

PHEBE tucks her head.

PHEBE   (*Flattered.*)

Go on.

AUGUSTUS   Tell me—how did you land
on the Jennings Plantation?

PHEBE   I didn't land at all. I was borned here.

AUGUSTUS   So this is your home.

PHEBE   Much as any of us got
a home on this earth.

AUGUSTUS   And your folks?

PHEBE   My father was sold before I was borned.
Mama...it's a long story.

AUGUSTUS   I got time.

*PHEBE stares down at the ground as if she's conjuring
the memory out of the dust; then she begins.*

PHEBE

Mama worked in the kitchen until
I was about five; that's when
fever broke out in the quarters.
She used to set table scraps out
for the field hands, and I
stuck wildflowers in the baskets
to pretty 'em up. Mama said
you never know what a flower can mean
to somebody in misery.

That fever tore through the cabins like wildfire.
Massa Jennings said the field hands
spread contamination and forbid them
to come up to the house, but
Mama couldn't stand watching them
just wasting away—so she started
sneaking food to the quarters at night.

Then the fever caught her too.
She couldn't hide it long.
And Massa Jennings found out.

Gulps a deep breath for strength, reliving the scene.

Mama started wailing right there at the stove.
Hadn't she been a good servant?
Who stayed up three nights straight
to keep Massa's baby girl among the living
when her own mother done left this world?
Who did he call when the fire
needed lighting? Who mended the pinafores
Miss Amalia was forever snagging on bushes?

Mama dropped to her knees
and stretched out her arms along the floor.
She didn't have nowheres to go;
she'd always been at the Big House.
"Where am I gonna lay
my poor sick head?" she asked.

He stood there, staring
like she was a rut in the road,
and he was trying to figure out
how to get round it.

Then he straightened his waistcoat
and said: "You have put me and my child
in the path of mortal danger,
and you dare ask me what to do
with your nappy black head?"
He didn't even look at her—
just spoke off into the air
like she was already a ghost.

Woodenly.

She died soon after.

AUGUSTUS takes PHEBE into his arms.

AUGUSTUS   (*A bit helplessly.*)

Lord have mercy.

PHEBE   Mercy had nothing to do with it.
Ain't that what you said?

AUGUSTUS   Phebe, how far would you go
to avenge your mother's death?

PHEBE   There you go again
with your revolution talk.

AUGUSTUS   How far?

PHEBE   We ain't got no tom-toms
like them slaves in Haiti!

AUGUSTUS You don't need tom-toms.
Just a bird call.

*PHEBE looks at him, uncomprehending. AUG-
USTUS stares off.*

*Stage dims to black: a single spot on the NAR-
RATOR.*

NARRATOR What is it about him, girl—
the book-learning, his acquaintance with
the world?
He can stand up to a glare,
but he doesn't know his heart.
Look around you, child: It's growing dark.

Scene 3

The cotton house.

Almost sundown: JONES is in the field supervising the bringing in of the cotton, which has been weighed and now must be tramped down in order to be stored. There is the steady beat of stomping feet throughout the scene. PHEBE and AUGUSTUS are outside the cotton house.

PHEBE   Any news?

AUGUSTUS   I expect another signal
               any day now. Then I'll know more.

PHEBE   What are they waiting for?
               You reckon something's gone wrong—

AUGUSTUS   (*Calming her.*)

               Shh. They have their reasons.
               Patience.

               PHEBE catches him looking at the sky.

PHEBE   (*With a mixture of jealousy and trepidation.*)

               You better get on up there—
               sun's almost touching.

               PHEBE scoots inside the cotton house. AUG-
               USTUS studies the horizon, his expression inexpli-
               cable, then exits as JONES enters from the fields,
               urging along the next group bearing cotton. The
               SLAVES are sweaty and tired. JONES looks
               after AUGUSTUS; it's clear he's been told not to
               interfere.

JONES

Keep it moving!
Don't be looking at the sun;
you got a whole long while
before your day is over!

*JONES exits. The scene opens to the inside of the
cotton house; SCIPIO dumps the sacks of cotton
onto the floor while the other SLAVES tramp it
down. The dull thud of stomping feet punctuates
the dialogue; changes in pace and rhythm signal
changes in mood and tension. On his way for the
next sack of cotton, SCIPIO looks out the one small
window.*

SCIPIO

There he goes.

ALEXANDER

Every evening, same time.

SCYLLA

It's the devil's work afoot, for sure.

SCIPIO

It *is* peculiar! I wonder—

PHEBE

It ain't your task to wonder.

SCIPIO

What's the matter with you, gal?
Most times you're the one speculating
about other folks' doings.
Maybe you're sweet on him.

General laughter.

PHEBE

If you ain't finding fault with someone,
you all laughing at them! We all been
called up to the house one time or another.
Ain't nothing special in that.

SCYLLA	For weeks on end? As soon as the sun eases into the sycamores, there ain't a hair of his to be seen till daylight.
	Significant pause.
	Except maybe on his lady's pillow.
PHEBE	What are you trying to say, Scylla?
SCYLLA	I ain't *trying* to say nothing.
ALEXANDER	He's certainly the boldest nigger I've ever seen.
SCIPIO	(*Shaking his head in admiration.*)
	That's the truth there! The way he handles Massa Jones— no bowing or scraping for him. That eye of his could cut through stone. Jones don't know what to do with that nigger! He's plain scared, and that's a fact.
PHEBE	Maybe they're just talking.
DIANA	Augustus is nice.
ALEXANDER	Nice as the devil was to Eve.
SCYLLA	A slave and his missus ain't got nothing to talk about. Oh, he might have bold ideas, but he'll never put them to work. She'll see to that.

PHEBE	What do you mean?
SCYLLA	That first master of his kept him in style. That's why he ran away so much afterwards— he ain't used to being treated like a regular slave. A whip can't make him behave: Miss Amalia knows that. So she's trying another way— and it appears to be working.
SCIPIO	Well, I'll be.
DIANA	What 'pears to be working?
SCYLLA	What's the only thing white folks think a nigger buck's good for? It wouldn't be the first time.
ALEXANDER	(*Slowly.*) If that's what he's doing, he's headed for big trouble.
PHEBE	I don't believe it! And even if it's true, it's 'cause he ain't got no choice!
SCYLLA	You been mighty contrary lately, Phebe.
PHEBE	I ain't afraid of every shadow!
SCIPIO	(*Trying to avert disaster.*) Scylla, don't mind her. She's feeling the weather.
SCYLLA	I'm warning you, Phebe.

PHEBE	I already got a pack of curses on my head. A few more won't hurt.
ALEXANDER	Phebe! Don't talk to Scylla like that!
PHEBE	Should have done it a long time ago. Woman had me nearly crazy! If anyone around here's putting sharp stones in my path, it ain't no earth spirit. If there's a curse here, Scylla, it's you.

Everyone stops stamping.

DIANA	Phebe...
PHEBE	Yes, Scylla, you're the curse— with all your roots and potions. Tell me: How come you never put a spell on Miss Amalia? Why didn't you sprinkle some powder over a candle to make her house go up in flames one night? That would have been some magic.

Timid murmurs from the others.

SCYLLA	I do what the spirits tell me.
PHEBE	Then those slaves in Haiti must have known some better spirits.
SCYLLA	Some nigger comes in here with a few pretty stories, and you think he's the Savior!
ALEXANDER	Dear Lord!

PHEBE   The Savior was never
                 to your liking, Scylla.
                 He took too much attention
                 away from you.

ALEXANDER   Have mercy!

SCYLLA   (*Drawing herself into her full "conjurer" posture.*)

                 There's a vine in the woods
                 with a leaf like a saw blade.
                 One side of the leaf is shiny dark
                 and pocked like skin;
                 the other side is dusty gray.
                 Touch the gray side to a wound,
                 the sore will shut and heal.
                 But touch it with the shiny side,
                 and the wound will boil up
                 and burst open.

PHEBE   Always talking in riddles!
                 Why don't you come right out and
                 say what you mean for a change?

                 *Agreeing murmurs; SCYLLA looks darkly
                 around until everyone grows silent.*

SCYLLA   Alright, I'll tell you direct.
                 Your Augustus is pretty clever—
                 been lots of places and knows
                 the meanings of words and things like that.
                 But something's foul in his blood,
                 and what's festering inside him
                 nothing this side of the living
                 can heal. A body hurting that bad
                 will do anything to get relief—anything.

                 Looking around at all of them.

So keep talking about Haiti
and sharpening your sticks!
But know one thing:
that nigger's headed for destruction,
and you're all headed there with him.

They stare at her as the lights dim to blackout.

Scene 4

The swamp.

Night: mottled light. Strangely twisted branches, replete with Spanish moss and vines; huge gnarled roots slick with wet. The whole resembles abstract gargoyles in a gothic cathedral. There's a gigantic tree trunk. At some re-move—in front of the proscenium, or silhouetted against the backdrop—the SLAVES pantomime the motions of evening chores: mending tools, shelling beans, stirring the stew.

When the lights come up, HECTOR is puttering around the perimeter of the swamp, muttering to himself; he finds a snake and lifts it up triumphantly before whacking off the head.

HECTOR   Hah! So many—under rocks, 'twixt reeds,
                                they lie and breed, breed, breed.
                                The wicked never rest.

                                Stops, listens.

                                What's that? Someone coming!

                                He scrambles for cover as HENRY and AUG-USTUS enter, stop, and shake hands.

HENRY   Good night, friend.
                                We will be victorious.

AUGUSTUS   May Fate be with us, brother.

HENRY   Oh she is, brother, she is.
                                It was a golden day
                                when Fate brought you to us.

They exchange the secret handshake; HENRY exits. AUGUSTUS looks after him; then, as soon as he thinks he's alone, he sinks down on a fallen log, burying his face in his hands. HECTOR—well hidden from AUGUSTUS but visible to the audience—looks on with keen interest; he recognizes this kind of despair. AUGUSTUS's soliloquy is more an agitated outpouring than a reflective speech.

AUGUSTUS   Compass and sextant. Ropes thick as my wrist,
coiled like greased snakes. A cutlass.
The rough caress of the anchor line slithering
between my boy palms. The hourglass tipped,
surrendering sand in a thin stream of sighs.
Clouded belly of the oil lamp dangling from a chain.
And everything rocking, rocking.

Hums a lullaby.

Dark green pillows, salve for my wounds.
"Who did this to you, boy?"
"It was the sun, Father; see its spokes?"
"Child of midnight, the sun can't hurt you!"

Sings softly.

"Jesus Savior pilot me
over life's tempestuous sea..."

Speaks.

And when she looks at me—
such a cool sweet look—
each scar weeps like an open wound.

Softer.

If fear eats out the heart,
what does love do?

HECTOR springs out of hiding; AUGUSTUS jumps up.

HECTOR   You! I've seen you before.

AUGUSTUS   (*Relieved.*)

                That you have, my friend.
                I'm from the Jennings Plantation, like you.

HECTOR   (*Stares at him suspiciously.*)

                Like me? Like me you say?
                We'll see about that.

                Circles him, inspecting.

                What are you doing in my swamp?

AUGUSTUS   Taking a walk. Breathing the night air.

HECTOR   Wrong! You were with someone.
                I saw you!

AUGUSTUS   Just a friend, Hector. Don't you have friends?

HECTOR   I saw you. I heard you!
                How do you know my name?

AUGUSTUS   We met before, don't you remember?
                I'm the new slave on the Jennings Plantation.

HECTOR   You're the one who came in leg irons,
                along the road—

                Circling him very closely, so that AUGUSTUS must back up.

                I never heard of leg irons on this plantation before.

Crowds AUGUSTUS, who trips on a root and falls.

You must be dangerous.

AUGUSTUS   I was sold in chains and spent my first night
in the barn. The overseer
didn't have enough sense to take them off
until Amalia gave the order—

HECTOR   Amalia? Amalia!
You are plotting some evil.

AUGUSTUS   You've got swamp fever, old man.
I plan no evil.

HECTOR   I heard you!
Men come and go in wagons.
They whisper and shake hands.
They come out at night
when the innocent sleep.

AUGUSTUS   These men—what do they look like?

HECTOR   They have the devil's eye.

AUGUSTUS   Are they black men, or white?

HECTOR   You are one of them!

AUGUSTUS   If they are black, black like
me and you, how can they be evil?

HECTOR   (*Vehemently.*)

No, no—the world's not right, don't you see?
I took the curse as far away as I could.

AUGUSTUS   There is no curse!

HECTOR   (*Draping moss and vines over the tree trunk to
                          make a "throne".*)

                          Ah, but the little mother's gone.
                          And I came here where evil
                          bubbles out of the ground.
                          Once I didn't watch out;
                          I got lost in the smell of a rose
                          and snap!—the snake bit down.
                          Little mother was mother no more.

AUGUSTUS   I'm no snake, Hector.

HECTOR   Evil isn't the snake, little man.
                          Evil is what grows the snake.

                          Gazing into the distance.

                          Such a cool sweet look...

                          *Cuts a piercing glance at AUGUSTUS, who
                          recognizes his own words and is on guard—
                          though against what, he's not sure.*

AUGUSTUS   You *are* crazy.

HECTOR   Once we had a garden to hide in,
                          but we were children.

                          *Taking his seat on the throne; with a full sweep
                          of his arm.*

                          This is my home now.
                          I am king here.

                          Regarding him suspiciously.

                          Every man has his place.

AUGUSTUS   And you are fortunate to have found yours.
                They've left you in peace.
                But what of your brothers and sisters?
                They cry out in their bondage.
                They have no place in this world
                to lay their heads.

HECTOR   (*In a low growl.*)

                You are planning a great evil.
                You come out at night
                when the innocent sleep—

                Raising his voice.

                but I won't let you harm her!

AUGUSTUS   Shh! Someone might hear.

HECTOR   I won't let you harm her!

                Screaming.

                Danger! Wake up, children!

                The SLAVES wake up and stumble out of their cabins, in a bewildered pantomime. The CONSPIRATORS also appear and consult each other.

AUGUSTUS   (*Grabbing HECTOR to silence him.*)

                Quiet! Do you want to bring
                the whole pack down on us?

HECTOR   (*Hits AUGUSTUS in the chest; crazed.*)

                Wake up! Wake up!
                Mother, Father!
                They're coming for us!

HECTOR tries to run out of the swamp.
AUGUSTUS tackles him from behind.

AUGUSTUS

Crazy fool! You'll spoil everything!
I've...come...to...save you!

A fierce struggle ensues.

HECTOR

(*In a vision from his childhood in Africa.*)

Fire! Fire!
The huts...the boats...
blood in the water.
Run, children, run!

AUGUSTUS gains control and kneels over HEC-
TOR, choking him; HECTOR gasps and is finally
still. When AUGUSTUS realizes HECTOR is
dead, he collapses on the lifeless body.

AUGUSTUS

Damn you, old man! I came to save you.

After a moment, he collects himself and stands up,
his voice breaking, more pitiful than angry.

Who is not with us, is against us.

HENRY

Selah.

The SLAVES begin humming as AUGUSTUS
kneels and wraps the body in vines, then rolls it
under a clump of moss and exposed roots.

AUGUSTUS

Let these vines be your shroud,
this moss a pillow for your head.
These roots will be your coffin,
this dark water your grave.

SLAVES	Selah.
AUGUSTUS	Sleep, Hector. Sleep and be free.

The SLAVES look at SCYLLA, who lifts her hand slowly.

SCYLLA	Eshu Elewa ogo gbogbo.

Blackout.

Scene 5

Lights rise on the NARRATOR.

NARRATOR   Sweet whispers can leave a bitter taste
                  when a body's supposed to be freedom bound.
                  Every day as the sun comes easing down,
                  our man climbs the stairs to sherry and lace.

Lights rise on the big house, LOUIS' study and the parlour.
Early evening. LOUIS sits hunched over his charts. He is excited.

LOUIS   Nothing in the books.
                  Empty sky in all the charts.
                  And yet I've seen it, with my own eyes!
                  Last night it was the brightest.

                  Draws a few lines with his compass, looks up wistfully.

                  What once was a void
                  fills with feverish matter.

                  LOUIS continues to fiddle with his papers throughout the
                  scene, occasionally jumping up to peer through the tele-
                  scope.

                  AMALIA stands by the fireplace, reading aloud from a
                  book.

AMALIA   The princess said to her father, "Bring me
                  strawberries, I am hungry for strawberries."

She shuts the book.

He came back with a husband instead.

Kneels before the fireplace, trying to start it.

"I'm getting too old to tend the garden,"
the king said. "Here is a husband for you—
he will fetch your strawberries."
The princess stomped her foot and replied
if she must have a husband,
she would rather marry the fox,
who at least knew where the sweetest berries grew.

And so she ran out of the palace
and into the woods, on and on
until a pebble in her shoe forced her to stop.
But it was not a pebble at all—
it was the king's head, shrunk to the size
of a pea.
"Put me in your pocket,"
the king pleaded, "and take me away with you."
Horrified, the princess threw the king's head down
and ran on. But she had not gone far
before she had to stop again,
and this time when she shook out her shoe,
it was the head of her husband that said:
"Please put me in your pocket
so that I may love you wherever you go."
The princess threw his head down, too,
and ran faster; but before long her shoe stopped her
for the third time. And this time
it was her own head she held in her hands.

She burns her hand, curses softly. There is a knock at the door.
An agitated JONES steps into the room, leaving the door
open.

JONES   Beg pardon for the disturbance, Ma'am,
                 but the matter's urgent.

                 *AMALIA rises, pulling her shawl tighter in
                 exasperation, and takes a seat behind the desk,
                 glaring.*

AMALIA   Since you've barged in, Mr. Jones,
                 the least you can do is close the door.
                 There's a chill; I believe I've caught it.

JONES   (*Closes the door, steps up to the desk.*)

                 Just what I wanted to talk to you about,
                 Miss Jennings. This cold spell—
                 it'll kill the last of the crops
                 if we don't get them in soon.

                 AMALIA doesn't respond.

                 Ma'am, you let the niggers
                 leave the fields early.

AMALIA   I thought you'd be happy, Mr. Jones.
                 Aren't such measures part of
                 your economic philosophy?

JONES   Not when there's cotton to be picked.

AMALIA   An hour more or less can hardly matter.
                 Now—this cold spell is unusual,
                 but not as threatening
                 as you make it out to be.

JONES   Well, the niggers sure are spooked.
                 They're just sitting around or looking off
                 in the sky. Matter of fact, they ain't even
                 been tending their own gardens.

AMALIA   This late in the season
                I don't imagine there's much left to tend.

JONES   And that crazy slave, the one's
                 got the shack out in the swamp—

AMALIA   Hector?

JONES   Yes'm, that's the one I mean.
                No one's seen hide nor hair of him.

AMALIA   Hector's in the habit of appearing
                whenever he has snakes to parade.

JONES   But it's been three days, Ma'am!

AMALIA   Cold weather makes the snakes scarce.
                Is that all, Jones?

JONES   Yes, Ma'am, as you please.
                Good evening, Miss Jennings.

                *JONES exits, closing the door behind him.
                AMALIA shakes herself once, briskly, as if try-
                ing to restore some measure of reason or calm.*

AMALIA   He's just waiting till the cold clears.
                He'll be alright.

                *Starts toward the window, stops to look in the
                mirror.*

                She looked down at her own head,
                cradling it in her cupped palms,
                and cried and cried herself to sleep
                beneath a giant oak tree.
                No one heard her. No one came.

AMALIA (con't.)	And so she perished, and her body was never found, even to this day.
	Listening.
	Augustus?
	AUGUSTUS enters, looking worn and pre-occupied. AMALIA runs to embrace him.
AMALIA	So you've come after all!
	Reaching out to stroke his chest.
	You look tired.
AUGUSTUS	(*Uncomfortable.*)
	I nearly collided with Jones, barrelling full steam across the porch.
AMALIA	Did he see you?
AUGUSTUS	Shadows are kind to niggers.
AMALIA	You're not a nigger!
AUGUSTUS	(*Catching her hand by the wrist.*)
	Yes I am, Amalia. Best not forget that.
AMALIA	(*Leading him to the fire.*)
	Come and get warm.
AUGUSTUS	(*Hanging back.*)
	What did Jones want?

AMALIA	Oh, he was complaining about the weather.
AUGUSTUS	The cold's hard on the crops. They should be picked fast.
AMALIA	(*Lightly.*) Scylla says the weather will break tomorrow.
AUGUSTUS	Since when have you taken to consulting Scylla?
AMALIA	I didn't "consult" her. She came up today and said, "If it please the Mistress, the cold has run its course. Morn will break warm, no worry."
AUGUSTUS	Why should you risk your profit on Scylla's words?
AMALIA	Look at us, squabbling about agriculture! Forget about the weather! Who cares what happens out there?
AUGUSTUS	Someone's got to care, Missy.
AMALIA	Don't call me that.
AUGUSTUS	That's what you are. And I'm your slave. Nothing has changed that.
AMALIA	(*Putting her hand to his mouth; AUGUSTUS withdraws, but only slightly.*) Shh! If this is all the world they've left us, then it's ours to make over. From time to time we can step out to show ourselves to the people so they will have someone to blame.

AUGUSTUS   It's too late.

AMALIA   Don't you think I see the suffering?
                  Don't you think I know I'm the cause?

                  With sarcasm and self-loathing.

                  But a master cannot allow himself
                  the privilege of sorrow. A master
                  must rule, or die.

AUGUSTUS   (*Pained, thinking of HECTOR.*)

                  Dying used to be such
                  a simple business. Easy—

                  Caresses her neck.

                  as long as there was
                  nothing to live for.

                  Tightening his grip; AMALIA shows no fear.

                  And murder simply a matter of being
                  on the right side of the knife.

AMALIA   (*Caressing him, pulling his shirt up.*)

                  Have you ever used a knife?
                  Have you ever killed someone?

AUGUSTUS   (*Haunted, evasive.*)

                  Now where would I get a knife?

                  *Turns abruptly away; from outside, barely audible,
                  come the opening strains of "Steal Away".*

AMALIA	(*Touching each scar on his back as she talks.*)
	Your back is like a book no-one can bear to read to the end— each angry gash, each proud welt... But these scars on your side are different.
	Touching them gently.
	They couldn't have come from a whipping. They're more like—more like markings that turn up in fairy tales of princes and paupers exchanged at birth.
AUGUSTUS	I've had them since birth.
AMALIA	(*Caressing him.*)
	So they are magical!
AUGUSTUS	Hardly—unless the art of survival is in your magician's bag of tricks.
	AUGUSTUS begins to return AMALIA's attentions.
AMALIA	They even look like crowns. Or suns—exploding suns! How did you come by them?
AUGUSTUS	(*Abrupt.*)
	No more stories.
AMALIA	Please?
AUGUSTUS	Another time. There's enough sorrow on earth tonight.

AUGUSTUS (con't.)   *Embracing her.*

                    And what's the harm in borrowing
                    a little happiness?

AMALIA   Take this, then—

                    Kisses him.

                    and this—

                    He pulls her down on the sofa as the strains of "Steal
                    Away" grow ever more urgent. AUGUSTUS
                    appears not to hear. He and AMALIA embrace pas-
                    sionately as the light dims.

Scene 6

In the slave cemetery.

HECTOR's funeral. HECTOR's body is lying in state on a crude platform, covered with a rough blanket. The SLAVES march around the bier as they sing. After a little while JONES enters and stands uncertainly in the background; AMALIA watches from her bedroom window.

LOUIS sits at his window but has turned his back. He stares into nothingness, brandy glass in hand.

SLAVES
> Oh Deat' him is a little man,
> And him goes from do' to do',
> Him kill some souls and him cripple up,
> And him lef' some souls to pray.
>
> Do Lord, remember me,
> Do Lord, remember me.
> I cry to the Lord as de year roll aroun',
> Lord, remember me.

ALEXANDER
> No children, and his kinfolk
> scattered around this world.

PHEBE
> We were all his friends, Alexander.

ALEXANDER
> But his youngest child's
> got to pass over and under!
> Who's going to do it?

PHEBE
> Every child on this plantation
> was like his child, Alexander.
> Don't you worry.

ALEXANDER   (*Breaking down.*)

                   To die like that, swoll up
                   and burst open like a—

PHEBE   He's at rest now. He don't feel it.

                   *The SLAVES stop marching to prepare for the ritual
                   of the "passing." In this rite, the youngest child of the
                   deceased is passed under and over the coffin to signify
                   the continuity of life.*

SLAVES   My fader's done wid de trouble o' de world,
                   Wid de trouble o' de world,
                   Wid de trouble o' de world,
                   My fader's done wid de trouble o' de world,
                   Outshine de sun.

                   *AUGUSTUS appears and he stands at a distance;
                   PHEBE goes over to him.*

ALEXANDER   Her he come, stopping by
                   when he's good and ready.
                   Too busy to pay proper respect to the dead.

SCIPIO   Each soul grieves in its own way.

PHEBE   Where were you?

AUGUSTUS   I came as soon as I heard—

PHEBE   (*Secretive.*)

                   Not here, man. There.

                   Gestures toward the swamp.

They were calling for you last night.
Didn't you hear that "Steal Away?"
They sang till I thought the dead
would rise out of their graves and follow!
I was crazy with worry.
Finally I went and told them
you couldn't get away.

*AUGUSTUS glances up at the house, locks gazes
with AMALIA.*

On the way back I tripped
over what I thought was an old root,
and there he was—

AUGUSTUS   *You* found him?

PHEBE   Under the crook of a mangrove,
wrapped in vines. Poor Hector!
All those years folks thought
he was crazy—

Looking up at AMALIA's window.

when he was just sick at heart.

ALEXANDER   Hector took a liking to you,
Diana. You should be the one.

*PHEBE joins the mourners as ALEXANDER
and SCIPIO pass DIANA under and over the
coffin.*

SLAVES   Lift him high, Lord,
Take him by the arm.
Wrap him in glory,
Dip him in balm.

AUGUSTUS kneels wearily. SCYLLA, ravaged with grief and more stooped than ever, approaches.

SCYLLA   He thought evil could be caught.

AUGUSTUS   Yes.

SCYLLA   But evil breeds inside, in the dark.
                I can smell its sour breath.

AUGUSTUS   Don't come around me, then.

SCYLLA   You believe you can cure the spirit
                just by riling it. What will
                these people do with your hate
                after you free them—as you promise?

AUGUSTUS   I got better things to do
                than argue with you, Scylla.

SCYLLA   Oh yes, you're a busy man;
                you got to watch for people waiting
                to trip you up; you think
                danger's on the outside.
                But do you know what's inside
                you, Augustus Newcastle?
                The seeds of the future; they'll have their way.
                You can't escape.
                You are in your skin wherever you go.

                Turns to the mourners, who have just completed the ritual of the passing, and calls out.

                Eshu Elewa ogo gbogbo!

ALEXANDER   He's gone over. He's flown on the wind.

SCYLLA	He came with no mother to soothe him. He came with no father to teach him. He came with no names for his gods.
PHEBE	No way but to see it through.
SCYLLA	Who can I talk to about his journey? He stood tall, so they bent his back. He found love, so they ate his heart. Eshu Elewa ogo gbogbo!
SCIPIO	This is what a man comes to.
SCYLLA	Who will remember him, without a father, without a mother?
PHEBE	Poor people, you've lost your wings.
SCYLLA	Eshu Elewa ogo gbogbo! Where are the old words now? Scattered by the wind.
ALEXANDER	The body a feather, the spirit a flame.
SCYLLA	And now the sun has come out to warm him.
SCIPIO	Too late! He's flown.
SCYLLA	But the wind won't carry me!
	The SLAVES hum and chant as they disperse, their song becoming gradually less mournful and more urgent as we segue into the next scene.
NARRATOR	Sunday evening; New moon, skies clear. The wheel's stopped turning: Redemption's here.

Scene 7

Near the slave cabins.

Early evening, shortly before sunset: PHEBE and AUGUSTUS come from the shadows. In the background the SLAVES go about evening chores while singing, a mixture of militant spirituals and African chants, with whispered phrases such as "Rise up!" or "Mean to be free!" occasionally audible.

AUGUSTUS	Everything's ready.
PHEBE	Yes.
AUGUSTUS	We've been careful.
PHEBE	Oh, yes.
AUGUSTUS	*(Pacing.)*
	Any day now. Any time!
PHEBE	It's been three days, Augustus— three days since you heard the call and didn't answer.
AUGUSTUS	Tonight's new moon; skies are clear. Destiny calls!
PHEBE	Are you sure it's not just your destiny?
AUGUSTUS	What do you mean?
PHEBE	Every time you talk about victory and vengeance, it's as if you're saying

my victory, my vengeance.
As if you didn't care about
anyone's pain but yours.

AUGUSTUS   Are you with us, or against us?

PHEBE   Ain't nothing wrong with feelings,
Augustus—just where they lead you.
Now when it comes to hating,
you and Miss Amalia are a lot alike.

AUGUSTUS whirls, but she stands her ground.

She used to be different—high-minded,
but always ready to laugh.
When she married Massa Louis
she began to sour.
Seemed like disappointment killed her.

Hesitates, then hurries through.

And now you've brought her back to life.
No wonder you're mixed up!

AUGUSTUS   Why are you telling me this?

PHEBE   Because I care what happens to you
more than revolution or freedom.
Those may be traitor's words, but
I don't care. 'Cause maybe—
maybe if you hadn't let hate
take over your life, you might have
had some love left over for me.

*She runs off. AUGUSTUS slowly sits down, as
if a new and treacherous path had opened before
him. BENJAMIN and HENRY enter unseen.
AUGUSTUS buries his face in his hands.*

BENJAMIN   (*Whispering.*)

                  There he is. Don't look
                  so fearful now, does he?

                  Makes a bird call.

AUGUSTUS   Who's there?

                  He leaps to his feet; the CONSPIRATORS approach.

BENJAMIN   May Fate be with you.

AUGUSTUS   You've brought news?

BENJAMIN   Most of the news is old, brother.

AUGUSTUS   It couldn't be helped;
                  I was under constant guard.

BENJAMIN   Constant guard? Constant companionship
                  would be closer to the truth.

AUGUSTUS   Talk straight!

BENJAMIN   Straight as a bullet, brother.
                  You sent word that you were "being watched"—
                  naturally, we sent someone to see about
                  your difficulties. What a surprise
                  to find out who your guard was
                  and how tenderly
                  she watched over you!

AUGUSTUS   Missy needed a buck—what of it?

BENJAMIN   Sound mighty proud, buck.

AUGUSTUS   Just the facts, brother, just the facts.
                Should I knock her hand away
                to prove my loyalty to the cause?
                Why not charm her instead?

BENJAMIN   That never used to be your style.

AUGUSTUS   I've never been so close to freedom.

BENJAMIN   All the more reason to see
                you don't spoil it.

                Looks skyward.

                The night's perfect:
                clear skies, new moon.

AUGUSTUS   Tonight? I knew it!
                I'll assemble my forces.

BENJAMIN   Hold on. You'll be coming with us.

AUGUSTUS   But—

BENJAMIN   You told us what you wanted us to believe.
                We've got orders to bring you to headquarters.
                They'll decide what's to be done.

AUGUSTUS   I can't leave. My people need me!

BENJAMIN   This is death's business, brother.
                Even a nigger as famous as you
                can't be given the benefit of the doubt!
                Your second-in-command—

AUGUSTUS   Phebe?

BENJAMIN   —will organize things here.

Takes AUGUSTUS by the arm.

Henry will deliver her orders.
We'll wait in the wagon. Come on!

*All exit; blackout. The chanting of the SLAVES
grows louder, with snatches of spirituals in high
descant, but the lyrics of the spirituals are vola-
tile. The percussive, more African-based chants
prevail, with key phrases like "Freedom, children,
freedom!" emerging ever stronger through the next
scene.*

Scene 8

The big house: AMALIA's bedroom, LOUIS' study and the hallway.

Evening: LOUIS stands at the open window of his study, looking through the telescope, alternately at the night sky and down over the plantation grounds.

AMALIA sits on the window seat in her bedroom. PHEBE enters.

PHEBE   You wanted me, Ma'am?

AMALIA   Good evening, Phebe!
                  I was sitting at the window,
                  catching the last rays of sunlight,
                  when I happened to see you
                  darting from group to group,
                  talking to this slave and that,
                  and I said to myself: "Perhaps
                  Phebe would like to talk to me, too."

PHEBE   (*On her guard.*)

                  I'm pleased to talk conversation
                  whenever you like, Miss Amalia.

AMALIA   (*Slightly sarcastic.*)

                  It seems you're mighty pleased
                  with other people's conversations
                  these days.

PHEBE   I don't follow your meaning, Ma'am.

AMALIA   Oh, really? I notice
              you and Augustus have no problem
              following each other's meaning.

PHEBE   Augustus ain't nothing
              but a friend, Ma'am.
              I don't recollect talking to him
              any more than anyone else.

              Laughs nervously.

              Me and my big mouth always be
              yakking at somebody or another.

AMALIA   Don't talk yourself
              into trouble, Phebe.

PHEBE   Beg pardon, Ma'am.
              I didn't mean nothing by it.

AMALIA   Everyone can see
              you're making a fool of yourself
              over him! Have you spoken
              to Augustus today?

PHEBE   I can't rightly say, Ma'am.

              At a warning look from AMALIA.

              That is—I talked to a lot of people
              and he was amongst them, but
              we didn't say more than a how-de-do.

AMALIA   Tell Augustus I want to see him.

PHEBE   (*Thrown into panic.*)

              I don't know—I mean—

AMALIA   What's the matter, Phebe?

PHEBE   Nothing, Ma'am.
                         It might take a while, is all.

AMALIA   (*Sarcastic.*)

                         And why is that?

PHEBE   It's just—well, Augustus been keeping
                         to himself lately. I seen him
                         going off in the direction of the swamp;
                         he's got some crazy idea
                         about fixing up Hector's shack.

AMALIA   (*Haunted.*)

                         Oh.
                         When he returns, send him up.

PHEBE   Yes, Ma'am.

                         *PHEBE exits. In the hallway she runs into
                         AUGUSTUS. He is very agitated.*

PHEBE   (*Whispering.*)

                         You! Here?

AUGUSTUS   Yes. They sent me back.

PHEBE   I thought for sure they was going to do
                         something awful to you.

AUGUSTUS   The sun travels its appointed track,
                         a knot of fire, day in day out—
                         what could be more awful?

PHEBE   Augustus, what is it?
               Can I help?

AUGUSTUS   This job I do alone.

PHEBE   But surely you can take a minute
               to go in there and smooth
               that she-hawk's feathers down
               so's the rest of us can—

               AMALIA steps out and peers into the dim hall.
               AUGUSTUS shrinks into the shadows.

AMALIA   Is that you, Phebe?

PHEBE   Yes'm. I was just on my way downstairs.

AMALIA   I heard voices.

PHEBE   That was me, Ma'am.
               I twisted my foot in the dark—
               guess I was talking to it.

               Laughs nervously.

               My mama used to say it helps
               to talk the hurt out.

AMALIA   Well, do your talking
               elsewhere. Go on!

               PHEBE hesitates, then exits. AMALIA stands look-
               ing into the darkness for a moment, then goes back into
               her room. AUGUSTUS steps out of hiding, holding a
               knife. The CONSPIRATORS can be heard in the
               background.

LEADER	Prove you haven't betrayed the cause!
BENJAMIN	Kill them both—
HENRY	— your mistress and her foolish husband.
AUGUSTUS	That's fate for you, Amalia.

Looks at the knife.

That white throat, bared for kisses...
one quick pass, and it will flow
redder than a thousand roses.

Everything was so simple before!
Hate and be hated.
But this—love or freedom—
is the devil's choice.

Steeling himself, he heads for LOUIS' room. Lights up on LOUIS, who is sitting with his right hand tucked nervously in the lap of his dressing gown. His back is to AUGUSTUS, who enters stealthily.

LOUIS   (*Startling AUGUSTUS, who stops in his tracks.*)

No-one has come through that door
for years. You're the new one, aren't you?

Unseen by AUGUSTUS, he pulls a pistol out of his lap.

A wild nigger, I hear. Amalia's latest indulgence.

AUGUSTUS   So this is the great white master,
trembling in his dressing gown!

LOUIS	Beware of the Moon in the house of Mars!
	Stands up and turns, hiding the pistol as he and AUGUSTUS face off.
	The stars can tell you everything— war and pestilence, love and betrayal.
AUGUSTUS	War? Yes, this is war. Say your prayers, Massa—you have a hard ride ahead of you.
LOUIS	A hard ride, me? I don't think so.
	Aims his pistol at AUGUSTUS.
	A man should be able to kill when he has to, don't you agree?
	Startled by this unexpected turn of events, AUGUSTUS freezes. LOUIS reaches for the bottle on the table with his other hand.
	Perhaps you'd care for a bit of bourbon to warm your way?
AUGUSTUS	(*Trying to compose himself.*)
	You can't stop what's coming over the hill.
LOUIS	(*Shakes his pistol at AUGUSTUS, shouting.*)
	This time I won't leave things up to chance!
	Muttering.
	What a fool I was! I should have smothered the bastard right there in the basket. That's the man's way.

AUGUSTUS   Basket? What basket?

LOUIS   Amalia's of course. Amalia's basket.
                It was—

                Slight pause; distracted.

                The doctor refused to kill it.
                What else was there to do?

                *AUGUSTUS lunges, knocking the gun from
                LOUIS' hand and overpowering him.*

AUGUSTUS   There goes your last chance, fool!

                Drags LOUIS by the collar toward center-stage.

                This basket—what did it look like?

LOUIS   What do you care?

AUGUSTUS   (*Holds the knife to LOUIS' throat.*)

                Enough to slit your throat.

LOUIS   (*Whimpering.*)

                Oh, it was beautiful! White wicker,
                lined in blue satin, tiny red rosettes
                marching along the rim...

AUGUSTUS   (*Slowly lets go of LOUIS' collar.*)

                And your spurs slipped right inside.

LOUIS   Amalia's Christmas present.
                Oh, was the good doctor relieved!
                "It's a miracle," he said,
                "but the child's still alive!"

AUGUSTUS   And still lives to this day.
               Spurs bite into a horse's belly—
               think what they can do
               to a newborn child!

               Rips open his shirt.

LOUIS   You?

AUGUSTUS   All my life I tried to imagine
               what you would look like.
               Would you be tall or stooped over?
               Blue eyes, or brown?
               Would you dress in white linen
               or dash around in a dusty greatcoat?
               to think that your blood flows
               through my veins—

               Advances on LOUIS, who staggers back into the chair.

LOUIS   My blood?

AUGUSTUS   When I think of you forcing
               your wretched seed into my mother,
               I want to rip you—

LOUIS   Me, your father?
               You think I'm your father?

AUGUSTUS   I heard it from your own lips.

LOUIS   (*Bursts into laughter.*)

               Of course! Of course!
               The stars said it all:
               who is born into violence

shall live to fulfill it.
Who shuns violence
will die by the sword.

AUGUSTUS   (*Pulls LOUIS from the chair, knife at this throat.*)

What happened to my mother?
What did you do to her?

LOUIS   (*In a crafty voice.*)

I haven't touched her since.
Ask Amalia—
she runs this plantation.
She knows your mother better than anyone!

AUGUSTUS   Amalia? Of course!
Missy wanted the bastard child dead.
Now I understand: It's an old story.

LOUIS   You understand nothing.

A sudden shout outside; the revolt has begun. Both men freeze, listening.

AUGUSTUS   It's time!

Stabs LOUIS as the sounds of the revolt grow.

LOUIS   You were there... all along...

AUGUSTUS   (*Letting LOUIS' body drop.*)

So, Amalia—and to think
I tried to bargain for your life!

SLAVES   Freedom! Freedom! Selah! Selah!

*AUGUSTUS heads for AMALIA's room; lights
come up on AMALIA, who has stepped into the hall.*

AMALIA   Augustus, there you are! What's happening?
          I called Ticey, but she won't come!

AUGUSTUS (*Backing her into the room.*)

          I thought you didn't care
          what happened out there.

AMALIA   Why are they shouting?
          Why doesn't Jones make them stop?

AUGUSTUS I reckon the dead don't make good overseers.
          Your slaves are rebelling, Missy.
          Liberté, Égalité, Fraternité!

AMALIA   (*Stares at him uncomprehendingly, then runs to the
          window.*)

          Rebelling? My slaves?
          Augustus, make them stop!
          They'll listen to you!

AUGUSTUS Like I listened to you?
          You led me into your parlour
          like a dog on a leash. Sit, dog!
          Heel! Care for a sherry? A fairy tale?

AMALIA   No, you were different!
          You were—

AUGUSTUS (*Grabs her.*)

          No more conversation!
          Where is my mother?

AMALIA   Your mother? How would I know a thing like that?

AUGUSTUS   Your husband confessed.

AMALIA   (*Aware of danger on all sides, seeking escape.*)

              What could Louis have to confess?

AUGUSTUS   A shrewd piece of planning,
              to destroy him with his own son
              after you had failed to destroy
              the son himself!
              But you had to be patient.
              Twenty years you had to wait
              before you could buy me back.

AMALIA   Louis, your father? You must be joking!

AUGUSTUS   Shall I help you remember?
              You supplied the basket yourself—

AMALIA   Basket?

AUGUSTUS   — lined in blue satin, trimmed with rosettes—

AMALIA   *Red* rosettes?

AUGUSTUS   Monsieur LaFarge agreed
              to sell his own baby—but that wasn't enough,
              was it? You wanted the child dead.
              So you slipped a pair of riding spurs
              into the sewing basket.
              And you know the kind of scars
              spurs leave, Missy. Like crowns...
              or exploding suns.

AMALIA   My God.

AUGUSTUS   The woman who patched me up
             kept that basket as a reminder.

AMALIA   No...

AUGUSTUS   (*Shakes her.*)

             What did you do with my mother?
             Who is she?

             Slaps her.

             Tell me!

AMALIA   (*Wrenches free to face him; her voice trembling.*)

             So you want to know who your mother is?
             You think, if I tell you,
             the sad tale of your life
             will find its storybook ending?
             Well then, this will be my last story—
             and when I have finished,
             you will wish you had never
             stroked my hair or kissed my mouth.
             You will wish you had no eyes to see
             or ears to hear. You will wish
             you had never been born.

AUGUSTUS   I've heard grown men scream,
             watched as the branding iron
             sank into their flesh. I've seen
             pregnant women slit open like melon,
             runaways staked to the ground
             and whipped until
             they floated in their own blood and piss.
             Don't think you can frighten me, Missy:
             Nothing your lips can tell
             can be worse than what
             these eyes have seen.

AMALIA	Bravo! What a speech! But you've seen nothing. *Backs up to appraise him, smiling, slightly delirious.* That same expression! How could I forget? My lover then stood as tall as you now.
AUGUSTUS	Your lover? *PHEBE bursts in.*
PHEBE	They're coming, Augustus! They're coming to see if you did what you were told! Oh, Augustus— you were supposed to kill her!
AUGUSTUS	(*Shaking himself into action, threatening AMALIA.*) My mother, who is my mother? Out with it!
AMALIA	Phebe, you tell him. You were there. Everyone was there— under my window, waiting for news...
PHEBE	That... was the night we all came to wait out the birth.
AUGUSTUS	What birth?
AMALIA	Hector on the porch.
AUGUSTUS	What about Hector? *More shouts outside; compelled by the urgency of the growing revolution, PHEBE tries to distract AUGUSTUS.*

PHEBE	There's no time!
AUGUSTUS	(*Grabs AMALIA as if to slit her throat.*)
	What about Hector?
AMALIA	Chick in a basket, going to market! They said you died, poor thing. That's why Hector went to the swamp.
	AUGUSTUS stares desperately at her. PHEBE turns, thunderstruck.
AUGUSTUS	Hector?
AMALIA	But you didn't die. You're here...
	Reaches for him; he draws back.
PHEBE	(*Looks from AMALIA to AUGUSTUS, horror growing, recites tonelessly.*)
	Stepped on a pin, the pin bent, and that's the way the story went.
AMALIA	(*Sadly, in a small voice.*)
	Silk for my prince, and a canopy of roses! You were so tiny—so sweet and tiny. I didn't know about the spurs.
PHEBE	You sold your own child. Hector's child.
AUGUSTUS	Hector...
	The knife slips from his fingers.

AMALIA   I was trying to save you!

AUGUSTUS   Save me?

AMALIA   (*Extremely agitated.*)

              I felt like they had hacked out my heart.
              But I wouldn't let them see me cry.

AUGUSTUS   (*Wrestling with the horror.*)

              You? My mother?

AMALIA   (*Clutching herself.*)

              It was like missing an arm or a leg
              that pains and throbs, even though
              you can look right where it was
              and see there's nothing left.

              She stops abruptly.

AUGUSTUS   My own mother gave me away.
              But I found my way back...
              a worm crawling into its hole.

AMALIA   For weeks afterwards
              my breasts ached with milk.

AUGUSTUS   (*Sinking to his knees.*)

              Better I had bled to death in that basket.

              *A great shout goes up as the insurrectionists gain en-
              try to the main house. AMALIA takes advantage
              of the ensuing distraction to pick up the knife.*

PHEBE   Augustus!

AUGUSTUS	(*Passive.*)
	The Day of Redemption is here.
PHEBE	They'll kill you, Augustus!
AUGUSTUS	Time to be free.
AMALIA	Poor baby! I thought I could keep you from harm— and here you are, right in harm's way.

PHEBE gasps; AMALIA stabs herself as AUG-USTUS, alerted by PHEBE's gasp, jumps up, too late to stop her. The room turns red as the out-buildings go up in flames.

AUGUSTUS	Amalia!

Catching her as she falls.

No...

Calling out in anguish.

Eshu Elewa ogo gbogbo!

The chanting of the rebelling SLAVES grows louder.

PHEBE	Oh, Augustus...
AUGUSTUS	(*Lays AMALIA's body down, gently.*)

I had the sun and the moon
once. And the stars

with their cool gaze.
Now it's dark.

PHEBE   It's alright. You'll be alright now.

AUGUSTUS   (*Staring as if trying to make out something in the distance.*)

Who's there? How she stares,
like a cat at midnight!

PHEBE   Nobody's there, Augustus.

AUGUSTUS   Don't you see her?

PHEBE shakes her head, terrified.

Look, she's hidden behind a tree.

PHEBE   Oh, Augus—

AUGUSTUS   Shh! You'll frighten her. There's another one—
he's been flogged and pickled in brine.
That skinny boy ate dirt; that's why he staggers.
So many of them, limping, with brands
on their cheeks! Oh, I can't bear it!

PHEBE   Come along, now.

AUGUSTUS   (*Calling out to the "ghosts".*)

I came to save you!

The SLAVES burst in, brandishing bayonets and torches.

BENJAMIN   He did it.

SLAVES	Selah! We're free!
	The SLAVES lift AUGUSTUS onto their shoulders. The SLAVE WOMAN/NARRATOR stands at the door, holding a torch, taking in the scene.
SLAVES	Freedom, freedom, freedom...

The "Freedom!" chant grows louder and more persistent as the SLAVES parade out of the room, AUGUSTUS on their shoulders; PHEBE follows them, sobbing. SCYLLA takes the torch from the SLAVE WOMAN/NARRATOR and sets fire to the window's billowing curtains as she slowly straightens up to her full height.

Blackout.

The End.

AN INTERVIEW WITH RITA DOVE

Conducted by Robert McDowell, Publisher of Story Line Press,

April 2000

Robert McDowell:

What are the differences between writing poetry and writing for the stage?

Rita Dove:

In an interesting way, poetry and drama are not that far apart. They seem much closer to me than poetry and novels, for instance, or even short stories. It's because of all the things you cannot say both in poetry and in drama — the fact that you know language is not enough, that it will never be enough. You go in there knowing that; you're armed with language, and it's all you have. So when I was writing this play, I almost never felt that I was in a strange country where I didn't know the landmarks. It wasn't quite a familiar landscape, but it wasn't really frightening; I could find my way. In poetry, there's so much you can't say because part of the task is to let the silence reverberate, to let each word mean everything that it can mean. In drama, you can't know what's running around in someone's head unless you write a soliloquy or an aside. So language-wise, the concerns and limitations are often very similar. While writing drama, I learned how to write a monologue, how much of the pacing of words and silence can be controlled at the script level. How many stage directions are enough, how much of the time and pacing I can orchestrate in a particular scene on the page, so that when I leave the play to a cast and director, it doesn't turn into something totally different.

The most challenging aspect of writing this drama for me, oddly enough, was the soliloquy. Poetry is all about interior thought; the theater tends to be about action. And yet the most critical dramatic passages are often those in which one character shares her thoughts with the audience. In my earliest versions of the play, no one had any monologues. It seemed unnatural to have a character simply talk to the audience. Even though poetry can be one long soliloquy, the tone of voice is often a whisper, a voice overheard rather than heard. That leap was a difficult one for me.

When writing plays, you have to keep asking yourself, How do I get this into the most streamlined form without being histri-onic? How do I pull the theatergoers into this world I am cre-ating? As a poet, I tend toward understatement and subtlety. As a playwright, I must find other modes of expression. When working on the play, I found it liberating to use utterance and movement in order to introduce subtlety into the play. There were things I could do that would not work in a poem because it would seem too — I don't want to say bombastic — but flamboyant. Like shouting.

The play came out of love of the theatrical space, where some human beings are illuminated on the stage, and others are in darkness, watching. You have an interplay of breaths; you have tension between moving bodies and those stilled bodies at-tending. I have always found the theater to be a magical space, and I have always longed to enter it in some way.

In the end, I discovered that poetry and drama have more in common than Aristotle, with his so-called "classic dramatic unities," may have cared to admit. Alfred Hitchcock once said that drama was "life with the dull bits cut out," and Gwendolyn Brooks defines poetry as "life distilled"— where's the big difference? For if a poet planes away unnecessary matter so that we can see clearly to the very core of the soul, a playwright commits the same sacred enterprise by training her spotlight on some select souls and then summoning the audience to listen, to bear witness in the dark.

Robert McDowell:

How did your musical training influence you?

Rita Dove:

I grew up with all kinds of music — blues and jazz and popular R & B. I have been actively involved in music since the age of ten, when I began playing the cello. Playing chamber music taught me the cadences of fugues and the power of harmony. I believe my poetry reflects an intense relationship to the music of the spoken word. Writing plays involves not only language but the interplay of various languages — different characters' varying speech patterns and inflections, personalities — as well as the visible rhythms of bodies relating to each other. A domestic scene in a play is like a string quartet.

Robert McDowell:

What literary and theatrical influences do you acknowledge?

Rita Dove:

When I was in grade school I began to imitate the satiric comic strips I was reading in Mad Magazine, which meant writing little plays involving my classmates and penning sardonic lyrics to popular tunes. During the summer vacations, my brother — who is two years older than me — and I would enact radio plays which we found in the public library; our father rigged up a microphone to the stereo system, and we tormented our parents with endless murder mysteries involving oriental temples (so we could bang a lid as a gong) and waterfalls (holding the microphone next to the running faucet). And then there was Shakespeare. Shakespeare was one of my earliest literary influences. I began reading the tragedies when I was about eleven years old. No one told me they were difficult, so I stumbled through them on my own, deliriously happy to have found such rich language, such musical utterances. I started with Macbeth because my mother was always quoting it while making dinner: "Is this a dagger which I see before me, / The handle toward my hand?" From there I went on to Julius Caesar, Othello and Hamlet.

High school browsing included Tennessee Williams and Adrienne Kennedy, who I thought was simply amazing. College added Ed Bullins and LeRoi Jones and Derek Walcott, as well as Elmer Rice's The Adding Machine, and all of Ionesco. I had nearly memorized Lorraine Hansberry's *A Raisin in the Sun* by that time, though I don't know exactly when I first read it.

Robert McDowell:

What difficulties can you share with readers regarding your adaptation of a classic?

Rita Dove:

Using the ancient Greek dramatic form, with its infamously difficult-to-handle master chorus, proved less problematic than I anticipated. I'd grown up in the black church, where call-and-response was part of the ritual. The black community extends beyond immediate family and even the neighborhood; it's a community that holds itself responsible for each member's actions and will feel free to voice its opinions — often loudly and with great sarcasm. So the type of running commentary provided by the Greek Chorus sounds "down home" to me!

Robert McDowell:

When did the inspiration for *The Darker Face of the Earth* come to you?

Rita Dove:

My husband and I spent five months in Jerusalem in 1979. I had recently finished the manuscript of my first book of poems, *The Yellow House on the Corner*, which contained a section of poems based on slave narratives, and I suppose that was on my mind one late afternoon that summer, as I stood looking out over the walled city of Jerusalem with its turrets and citadels. I had just reread Sophocles' Oedipus Rex; and perhaps it was the natural amphitheater of the Kidron valley, where King David cried out at the loss of his rebellious son Absalom, perhaps it was the slanted sunbeams striking the pale stones of the Old City like a spotlight dressed with the palest of pink gels — but I found myself musing on kings and all-too-human heartbreaks, looking for similarities between the classical sense of destiny and our contemporary attitudes toward history and its heroes. What is it, I wondered, that makes Oedipus interesting as a hero when his course has been set at birth? Why do we watch, enthralled, if we already know his fate? I searched for a modern analogy, a set of circumstances where the social structure was as rigid and all-powerful as the Greek universe, one against which even the noblest of characters would be powerless. And as the sun began to set behind the Mount of Olives, a Jimmy Cliff song floated from my husband's study:

> *Oh de wicked carry us away,*
> *Captivity require of us a song;*
> *How can we sing King Alpha's song*
> *In a strange land?*

The lines are adapted from Psalm 137, the cries of the Israelites in bondage — but sung, in Cliff's version, by the slaves in the Americas.

And there I had my analogy. Rarely has history seen a system which fostered such a sense of futility as slavery. For the Africans taken forcibly from their homes and their roots — language, family, tribal memory — systematically decimated, the white power structure must have seemed as all-encompassing as the implacable will of Zeus. In a flash, I had the basic constructs: A child born of a white plantation mistress and her African lover is sold off but returns twenty years later, unaware of his origins. The open secret of miscegenation would be the key that turns the lock of Fate, and instead of Tiresius, a conjure woman would prophesy the curse. Pride and rebellious spirit have little chance in the systemic violence of slavery, which brutalizes both slave and master: In a different world, Amalia might have been a woman of independent means and Augustus a poet; instead, both are doomed to be crushed when their emotions run counter to the ruling status quo. The slaves know this and function as a Greek chorus, commenting and warning, all to no avail.

Robert McDowell:

This was in 1979 — but the play wouldn't see the light of day until 1994. What happened?

Rita Dove:

I wrote the first draft of the play in less than a month, but it would take a dozen or so years before I arrived at a version that I felt was ready to be shown to the world. I dutifully sent a few copies of that first draft to New York agents, knowing that it was everything a play couldn't be to succeed in the commercial theater world: a historical drama, an adaptation of a Classic with too many non-mainstream characters. When the copies came back (some accompanied by encouraging but no-thanks notes), I put them in a drawer and went on with my life in poetry. Every five years or so my husband would drag out the manuscript and ask, "What are you planning to do with this?" I'd look at it, try to take out a few characters, maybe shuffle them around a bit, and put it away again. The next time I'd rewrite it as prose, then put it back in the drawer. Finally in 1989, I took a long hard look at the play, said, "What the hell," and put it back into verse. Who cared if it never got published? At least when I was dead and gone, the version scholars would find among my papers would be the one I wanted them to see.

Story Line Press published that version of *The Darker Face of the Earth* in early 1994. I still held no hopes for a production, but I thought it would be nice for literature studies — and maybe it would even get some exposure in staged readings like the one the Washington, D.C. director Jennifer Nelson—who had read the play in script—was able to arrange at the Round-house Theater in Silver Springs, Maryland shortly after publication. But as it turned out, a board member of the Oregon Shakespeare Festival had gotten a copy of the galleys in her hands and recommended it to the Festival dramaturg, and before I knew it, OSF offered to workshop it with a first production option. They hired Jennifer Nelson to direct the workshop, and so I spent three weeks in Ashland, Oregon that summer watching my scenes come to life — some more, some less — in a rehearsal room, discussing, rewriting, making notes for possible changes to mull over later. At about that time the dramaturg of Crossroads Theatre in New Brunswick, New Jersey came across the play in a bookstore, and Crossroads approached the Oregon Shakespeare Festival to offer a pooling of resources. The play was first produced in Oregon in the summer of 1996, directed by Crossroads artistic director Ricardo Khan. By that time I had rewritten it, mostly on the basis of my experiences during the OSF workshop but also in response to several staged readings — among them the wonderful one that Derek Walcott directed in November 1995 at the 92nd Street "Y" in New York City, where Walcott and his talented cast brought out the full potential of what I was trying to say. Crossroads then staged *The Darker Face of the Earth* in the fall of 1997; they had submitted it to the Fund for New American Plays at the Kennedy Center and been granted major financial support from the Fund, which in turn led to a month-long run in Washington, D.C. right after the New Brunswick shows.

Robert McDowell:

Please tell us more about the productions the play has had so far. Your favorite?

Rita Dove:

The play has seen four professional productions to date (as of spring 2000), all at major not-for-profit theaters, and several college productions, with at least two more professional and maybe half a dozen college stagings under contract. The world premiere, July to October 1996 at the Oregon Shakespeare Festival, remains my favorite. The 600-seat Angus Bowmer Theater in Ashland, Oregon is a semi-thrust stage built so ingeniously that every seat affords an unobstructed view; as an audience member one feels quite intimately involved with the action on stage even while being treated to a vision of a stage "set". And the set design, by Richard Hay (who, incidentally, is also the architect of the Bowmer Theater) was stupendous. It was the production I felt kept the best balance when exploring dramatic "effects" while remaining faithful to the spirit of the text and even the integrity of the lines. The actors were superbly cast, the artistic staff dedicated and fearless, the technical people topnotch. Every performance was met with a standing ovation, sometimes foot stomping and cheers. Some people were weeping so hard at the end that they actually had to be helped out of their seats by the ushers. Nothing can equal that experience!

Crossroads Theatre put up the next production a year later in their space in New Brunswick, New Jersey, again directed by Ricardo Khan. Crossroads has a three-quarter thrust stage in a very small space — approximately 260 seats — which made for very intimate theater indeed. The play was very accessible in that space, and the audience was so actively engaged that some people actually blurted out advice to characters on-stage! That same production — set, cast and all — was then transferred in less than three days to the Kennedy Center, where it played for a month on the huge proscenium stage of the 1200-seat Eisenhower Theater. Talk about rapid adjustment! And needless to say, this transfer to a vastly different space caused some problems of its own.

I was less than pleased with the production at the Royal National Theatre in London, England in the summer of 1999. It was staged "in the round," with the audience looking down on the set from all four sides, which not only obscured sight lines for huge chunks of the audience but actually worked against the narrative thrust. The director disregarded my input while I was present during the last three weeks of rehearsals; he even tried to manipulate my text! By opening night we were no longer on speaking terms, and the actors were primed to stage a little insurrection of their own.

The most recent production (in March 2000) occurred at the Guthrie Theatre in Minneapolis. It offered a good cast and a talented director, but it could have been stronger had the Guthrie allotted more rehearsal time —it had only four weeks instead of the six to eight at the other professional productions. The short rehearsal period made it hard for the director to adjust problems of blocking, timing, etc. in such a complex drama. Also, in my view the set design was unfortunate, with the most intimate scenes — in the bedroom and the parlor — situated the furthest away from the audience . . . and that in a 1300-seat house! Overbearing choreography contributed to the alienation and slowed the action instead of accelerating it.

A pleasant surprise was a college production in Oberlin, Ohio in the spring of 1999. Caroline Jackson Smith, a professor of theater there, proved to be a congenial director, utilizing a well thought-out set design to direct a powerful interpretation that, cast with professional actors, I believe could have done Broadway proud.

Robert McDowell:

Are you working on another play?

Rita Dove:

Right now I'm working on several things — poems, a memoir, a novel. I've started two theater projects: one is a full length play, the other an evening of one-acts with interrelated characters. Let's wait and see.

THREE DIFFERENT APPROACHES TO TEACHING AND STUDYING RITA DOVE'S *THE DARKER FACE OF THE EARTH*

I. Literary Analysis, English 220

Taught by Ann M. Fox, Assistant Professor of English at Davidson College in Davidson, North Carolina.

One way to read Rita Dove's *The Darker Face of the Earth* is as an adaptation of Sophocles' *Oedipus Rex*. In an essay compare the two, discussing how and why Dove makes this intertextual link. Explore what you think the one or two major themes of Dove's play are, and why/how she makes use of Sophocles' play to convey these. Is it effective? Important? In addition, explore the major ways in which Dove's play differs from the Greek original, and why those differences matter in light of the literary ends you've attributed to Dove. Find specific examples that support your conclusions.

The above exam essay might be a good starting point for classes that have already read *Oedipus Rex*. However, it is important to talk about other issues that branch off from that comparison:

CANONICITY

- Why do you think Dove models her play—a play by an African-American woman, one speaking very specifically to the slave experience in this country—on a canonical work of Greek theater?
- What is the significance of placing her play in dialogue with others that have long been considered "timeless"?
- Does she challenge canonical standards of drama? Revise them? Reinforce them?
- To what extent can this play still be seen as an outgrowth of an African-American tradition of theatre in staging and/or theme?

CANONICITY (Continued)

- You might also compare her use of poetic diction to the innovative language used by playwrights like Ntozake Shange, for example.

DOVE'S REVISION

- What does it mean that our "Oedipus" figure is carried off in triumph in the end?
- Does this play still end tragically? How?
- While there are certainly many slave narratives yet to be told, this is not the first work of literature to depict the slave experience. Why does Dove historicize her work in this way?

ANALOGIES TO CONTEMPORARY LIFE

- Are there analogies to be drawn between the play to contemporary African-American life?
- What about African-American culture—its traditions, its history, its rituals—is Dove trying to represent?

SOCIAL STRUCTURE

- In what ways does the destructive power of privilege become exposed in the play?
- Is Amalia a victim or an oppressor? How is she both?
- Are there connections to be drawn between her fate and her son's?
- To what extent are the economics of slaveholding—as well as the economics of marriage—operant as insidious "fates" in the play?
- In what ways is the world of the plantation a microcosm for the world beyond its gates—as well as our own world, today?

POWER REVERSALS

- What are we to make of the power reversals in the play, e.g., of the fact that our father figures (Hector and Louis) are both ineffectual, if not mad?
- Why does Dove invert race and gender power relationships in the world of this play?
- Is it any less insidious when Amalia claims Augustus' body sexually than when male slaveowners would rape their female slaves?

DESIGNING THE PLAY

- How would you design a production of this play?
- Could it be cast cross-racially?

FURTHER TOPICS for discussion and exploration

- Sexism/racism
- Use of offstage characters
- Significance of the play's final scene/final image
- Experimentation (either in form or theme)
- Parents and children
- The use of songs
- Fate/ the 'curse'
- Sexuality
- Coming of age
- Revolution
- Interracial relationships
- Religion

II. English 20: Exposition and Argument

Taught by Marjorie Rubright, Graduate Teaching Assistant at the University of Missouri-Columbia in Columbia, Missouri.

Research Assignment: Dove's play treats as themes a wealth of historical topics that students enjoy exploring. This assignment begins with a close reading of the play and then requires significant research into some aspect of America's history with slavery. The paper asks the students to return to the play and to bring their research to bear on their own careful analysis of one of the themes in *The Darker Face of the Earth*.

A. CHOOSING A TOPIC

Sample Topics
- voodoo
- slave songs
- important rites and rituals of slaves
- education of slaves
- sexual relations between slaves and masters
- interracial children born into slavery
- underground railroad

By no means is this list exhaustive. Your reading should engender further topics.

Write a one paragraph response to the following questions:

- What theme in the play have you chosen as your topic?
- Is your topic primarily connected to one character in the play? If so, who is that character and how is he/she connected or involved with that topic/theme?
- If not, who are the characters and how are they connected to or involved with the topic/theme?

Block quote a short passage from the play in which your topic appears and answer the following question:

- What historical information would you like to have in order to more fully understand the moment you cite? How might having more historical information shed light on your interpretation(s) of this pasage?

List three questions that you have about your topic as it appears in the passage you cite.

B. ANNOTATED BIBLIOGRAPHY AND RESEARCH LOG

For this part of the assignment you will be conducting historical research on your topic. Hand in an Annotated Bibliography of at least three sources which may include:

- An article of 7 or more pages
- One chapter of a book

While the use of encyclopedia entries, brief magazine articles, internet resources and reference books may serve as excellent starting points—your three annotated sources must be from scholarly journals. If you have a question about a source consult a reference librarian or your professor.

Bring your Research Log to class.

C. PAPER

The Darker Face of the Earth is being produced in Atlanta for an audience well informed about the history of slavery. The themes that arise in Dove's play will not only be familiar to that audience, but the critic who will review the play on opening night is an expert on your topic. The director hopes for a positive review but knows that if an actor does not fully understand his/her role within the historical contexts that apply to that role, this critic will not offer favorable reviews.

The director has asked you to give a talk to either:
• One character who is most closely associated with your topic
• The actors involved in one act of the play in which your topic is a primary theme of that act

The director has asked that you aim not to regurgitate facts from the history books (because her actors can read those books themselves). She does not want a "history report." She has hired you to explore why the historical information regarding your topic is important to the actor's interpretation of his or her role and how having the historical information affects the choices the actor will make as he/she plays the role.

ASSIGNMENT NOTES

The open-endedness of the question is intentional. The question for the final essay (part C) engenders a variety of approaches to the paper. Some students have written papers in speech form, as if they were going to deliver their paper to actors. Other students prefer a more traditional, thesis-driven essay approach.

The range of topics that this assignment encourages is part of the pleasure of teaching this text and part of the students' pleasure when they read one another's papers. Many students have written essays on how slave songs function as code-language on the plantation. One student, for example, explored the moment that Augustus remains in the house with Amalia despite the slaves' increased singing as the moment of crisis in the play. This student explored the history of how slave songs were used as coded speech, allowing communication between individuals on a plantation as well as communication between plantations. This research came to bear on her assertion that Augustus's decision to stay in the home when the slaves called him back to the plantation is central to the drama of Augustus's interracial identity.

OTHER ESSAY TOPICS

- The complicated relationship between Hector and Amalia
- The snake cults in African religions
- The multiple biblical as well as African-based religious connotations of Hector's seeming obsession with killing snakes
- The association of voodooism with Skylla
- How voodoo coexists with the "master's" religion

RECOMMENDED SUPPLEMENTAL READING

- *The Slave Community: Plantation Life in the Antebellum South.* John W. Blassingame
- *Africans in America:America's Journey through Slavery.* Charles Johnson & Patricia Smith
- *Narrative of the Life of Frederick Douglass. An American Slave.* Frederick Douglass
- *Incidents in the Life of a Slave Girl.* Harriet Jacobs
- *White Women, Black Men: Illicit Sex in the Nineteenth-Century South.* Martha Hodes
- *Black Slave Narratives.* John Bayliss
- *Mistresses and Slaves: Plantation Women in South Carolina.* Marli Weiner
- *"When I Can Read my Title Clear": Literacy, Slavery, and Religion in the Antebellum South.* Janet Duitsman Cornelius

III. English 129: The European Literary Tradition

Taught by Diana R. Paulin, Assistant Professor of American Studies and English at Yale University in New Haven, Connecticut.

Another approach to Rita Dove's play is to study it in the context of the European tradition and ask why this play also works when placed in the U.S. antebellum context. Think about the ways in which the play addresses both "universal" questions about familial dynamics and taboos, as well as particular aspects of U.S. history (such as, slavery, miscegenation, and the cult of true womanhood). Also, look at how Dove's position as poet laureate informs her role as a national storyteller, similar to Greek epic poets, and influences her decision to use this narrative to play out the "drama" of slavery and rebellion in the U.S.

POINTS TO PONDER

- Why does Dove choose this form (The Oedipal myth/Sophocles' *Oedipus Rex*) to tell this story?
- What U.S. (racial, national, familial) mythologies does she draw from/invoke?
- How does her play and her strategy for telling her story resonate with other tragic plays, both classical and modern? (alienation of audience, ends with rebellion, fall fo tragic hero, etc.)
- What does Dove transform/change in her play?
- What category would you put this play in? (tragedy? melodrama?) Why?
- How does she both incorporate and transform/revise the "tragic mulatto" convention from 19th and early 20th century narratives?
- What is the importance of repetition in the play?
- How is fate tied in with the inevitability of the violent ending? In terms of rebellion? Suicide? Impending Civil War?
- What African retentions does she insert into the play?
- How does her play challenge more conventional formulations of race and gender?

POSSIBLE PAPER TOPICS

- Compare the different versions (1st and 2nd editions) of the play. What changes were made and how does this shape the story and the way in which it emphasizes certain aspects of the tragedy over others?
- How does Dove transform classical formulations of gender in her modern articulation of the Oedipus tragedy?
- How does race and the history of race relations in the U.S. inform Dove's retelling of this classic or "universal" tale?
- Talk about the redemptive possibilities of Rita Dove's play. How does her conclusion invite multiple interpretations of the racial drama represented in *Darker Face?*

SUPPLEMENTAL TEXTS/PLAYS

- Berzon, Judith R. *Neither White Nor Black: The Mulatto Character in American Fiction.* New York: NYU Press, 1978.
- Boucicault, Dion. *The Octoroon.* 1859. *Best Plays of the Early American Theatre: From the Beginning to 1916.* Ed. John Gassner. New York: Crown Publishing, 1967. 185 - 215.
- Fabre, Genevieve. *Drumbeats, Masks and Metaphor.* Cambridge: Harvard University Press, 1983.
- Hughes, Langston. *Mulatto.* 1935. *Black Theatre U.S.A: Plays by African Americans, The Recent Period: 1935 - Today.* Revised and Expanded Edition. New York: The Free Press, 1996. Ed. James V. Hatch and Ted Shine. New York: The Free Press, 1996. 4-23.
- Johnson, Georgia Douglas. *Blue Blood.* 1926. *Black Female Playwrights: An Anthology of Plays before 1950.* Ed. Kathy A. Perkins. Bloomington: Indiana UP, 1989. 38-46.
- Johnson, Georgia Douglas. *Blue-Eyed Black Boy.* 1935-1939. *Black Female Playwrights: An Anthology of Plays before 1950.* Ed. Kathy A. Perkins. Bloomington: Indiana UP, 1989. 47-51.

THE AUTHOR

The Darker Face of the Earth is Rita Dove's first full-length play. It received major grants from the Fund for New American Plays, the W. Alton Jones Foundation, the Geraldine Dodge Foundation and the National Endowment for the Arts and premiered at the Oregon Shakespeare Festival in 1996. It has been staged at Crossroads Theatre, the Kennedy Center, the Royal National Theatre in London, the Guthrie Theater in Minneapolis, the Fountain Theatre in Los Angeles, and other theatres.

Rita Dove served as Poet Laureate of the United States and Consultant to the Library of Congress from 1993 to 1995 and was reappointed Special Consultant in Poetry for 1999/2000, the Library of Congress's bicentennial year. Born in Akron, Ohio in 1952 and a 1970 Presidential Scholar as one of the 100 best U.S. high school graduates that year, she received her B.A. summa cum laude from Miami University of Ohio and her M.F.A. from the University of Iowa, and she held a Fulbright scholarship at Universität Tübingen in Germany. She has published seven poetry collections, among them *Thomas and Beulah*, for which she was awarded the 1987 Pulitzer Prize, and most recently *On the Bus with Rosa Parks* (1999). She is also the author of a book of short stories and the novel *Through the Ivory Gate*. Her song cycle Seven for Luck, with music by John Williams, was premiered by the Boston Symphony Orchestra in 1998, and she collaborated with John Williams on Steven Spielberg's documentary The Unfinished Journey for "America's Millenium."

Rita Dove's honors include, most recently, the 1996 Heinz Award, the 1996 Charles Frankel Prize/ National Humantities Medal, the 1997 Sara Lee Frontrunner Award, the 1997 Barnes & Noble Writers for Writers Award and the 1998 Levinson Prize. She is Commonwealth Professor of English at the Unversity of Virginia in Charlottesville, and she writes a weekly column "Poet's Choice," for the Washington Post. Up-to-date biographical information is available on her web site under "http://www.people.virginia.edu/~rfd4b/".